About the author:

I0081013

Matthias Leue is a fine art photographer and writer based in Oakland, California.

He grew up moving several times between the United States and his native Germany. He was born in Köln, Germany, lived in Philadelphia on the East Coast, then in Frankfurt, Germany, on the Monterey Peninsula, and in the San Francisco Bay Area here in California.

"Sea Shells, *C'est Gratuit*" is his second published book.

Other Books by Matthias Leue

Fish Camping And Other Travel Stories

SEA SHELLS

C'EST GRATUIT

SEA SHELLS

C'EST GRATUIT

MATTHIAS LEUE

First Edition, December 2013

© 2013 by Matthias Leue

Published by Flatfish Books
Oakland, California
www.flatfish-books.com

Drawings of black cat, raccoon face, sparrows, river fish, full moon over France, cactus flower, Arc de Triomphe, La Merci Dieu, dog, Easter egg, and duck: Anne Leue
Drawings of kissing fish and speeding koi: Christian Leue
Watercolors of Trouville on the cover, Carmel Valley, Clay-Souilly, Gare de Lyon, Joshua Tree, Phoenix, Thüringen, and book design: Matthias Leue
Drawings of linden tree, fish ladder, blue jay, honey jar, and taxi wreck: Patrick Leue
Author photo: Gary Hunt
Editor: Susan Swerdlow

If you are not satisfied with these conditions, do not attempt to turn the page.

ISBN 13 978-0-9835351-1-9
Library of Congress Control Number: 2013931703
Library of Congress subject headings:
European Union countries -- Description and travel, humor
United States -- Description and travel, humor
Travelers' writings
Special Interest, adventure

This book is dedicated to the glory of God.

About this book:

"Sea Shells, *C'est Gratuit*" is technically speaking, my second book. It is a color version of my book "Fish Camping" to showcase the watercolors and drawings. It also contains one additional story with current observations of my neighborhood and surroundings here in the Oakland, California. The story "My Oakland Neighborhood" was written in 2012. Chronologically speaking, my first book, which is a cookbook, spanning the years 1988 to 1996, is still a bit delayed; please be patient, I'm working on it. The time frame for "Sea Shells, *C'est Gratuit*" is about the years 1996 to 2002. This collection of travel stories is primarily about my sons Christian and Patrick, my extended family, and my friends. When I first started to write these stories, I always jotted down notes whenever I had the chance to travel some-where, which was usually during summers to see family and relatives in Germany and France. Eventually, these notes became travel stories, which grew more expansive as time went by and proficiency increased. I hope this compilation of travel stories and my attempts at humor bring a little joy as well as maybe some encouragement into your life and bring back some memories for the people I have written about. I'm a bit of a dreamer and romantic, which may be reflected in this work.

Matthias Leue

Another special thank you to my editor Susan, who has the eyes of an eagle

Story Index

SEA SHELLS

C'EST GRATUIT

Camping at Juniper
Spring 1996

Where is that camp stove? I'm tired and stressed on Friday after work, having been confined to a cubicle in a temp job. I decide to head to my humble abode, pack my futon, the aforementioned camp stove, a sleeping bag and a few groceries into my truck, and head out to relax for a night in the great outdoors.

Allow me to share a discovered camping spot with a panoramic view: Mt. Diablo, named (or misnamed, one might say) during the 1804 colonization days of the Spanish military, and the tallest peak in the San Francisco Bay Area. The mountain is only half an hour past Walnut Creek and has several campgrounds perched on it. Juniper is the name of my personal campground preference and it is located near the peak. From there you can watch the sunset and see pretty much the entire Bay Area below you, on a clear day.

The sun has left for the day, and it quickly gets cool as a breeze caresses the mountain, while the Big Dipper and its compatriots start to sparkle in the night sky. After a small meal prepared on the stove (spaghetti Bolognese this time) and a hot cup of coffee, the stress of "civilization" slowly dissipates. Forgotten is the solitary confinement

of the cubicle. I quickly fall asleep, but awaken in the middle of night to the sound of clack-clack-plop, clack-clack-plop. I climb out of the truck bed and walk towards the picnic table to investigate the sound. I see a raccoon, medium of stature, lifting up the flaps of my picnic basket in obvious search of edible delights. The surprise is mutual, and he, for one, decides to depart. Spoil-sport that I surely am, I place the picnic basket under the table where it cannot be opened, and go back to sleep. I imagine this night-time procedure has been duly noted from a distance, probably no doubt with much contempt.

I awake early to the sound of the other half of the scavenger tandem indigenous to this mountain, the scrub jays. They have the habit of perching on the highest treetops and don't miss a wink when it comes to food. The greed-fear factor on their part seems always proportionate to the distance they are from anything edible and how fast the location can be approached by the defender of said groceries, in this case yours truly. I get up to fix breakfast and walk over to the picnic table. And what do I see? Several opened packages of instant soup scattered about and around the picnic basket. So someone was back after all when I fell asleep again, and it seems that my wedging the basket under the table was a poor preventive measure. I suppose the masked bandit will have to wait until the rainy season to reap the full benefits of his misdeed when instant turns to soup.

La Merci Dieu
Summer 1996

After a long drive through Germany, Belgium, and France, we arrive at La Merci Dieu, which lies in the countryside about three hours southwest of Paris, and are greeted by a wonderful light evening summer meal. At the door of the grand old house, hundreds of moths flutter with abandon around the entrance light. They have a peculiarity about them that despite their inland habitat, they smell like the ocean. Odd. I make my way up the stone staircase and past several hallways to find my room, ducking under a petrified bat in an archway while smelling the dampness of the thick stone walls of the old *château*. Meanwhile the kids, armed with flashlights, get to know French soil under the tent they have set up outside for the night. I soon fall asleep to the hoots of an owl.

We wake up the next morning to *café au lait* and fresh bread and home-made jam. The French have a way of turning morning into a delight. Properly fed, we help to carry and reroute irrigation pipes to the fields outside. Many hands make light work. Returning, we set up tables outside for lunch, including a small one for the children. Another wonderful summer meal prepared by Madame du Hamel and one of her daughters, Cécile, fills the tables. The conversation is in French, of course, but the warmth and peace transcend language barriers.

Dinner is another delight, and the moths and bats keep us company again. One of the summer pleasures here is that it stays light late.

We spend the next day exploring the river that flows behind the old *château*. Patrick makes a fishing pole out of bamboo he finds growing by the river. Unfortunately, the fish do not cooperate, despite his effort. Not very sporting of them, if you ask me. We decide to play with Jelly, a black and white mutt. She has the amusing habit of devouring plums, all that are in her reach on the plum tree and ones that are fed to her. She is always the first under the kids table once meals are finished, knowing where scraps are to be found.

Bats fly across the night sky once again during our second evening's dinner. Bugs beware, you are no match for them.

The next morning we drive to a very old stone church in one of the neighboring villages to attend service. Hymns echo inside the old walls. Afterwards, people stop to pick up fresh bread from the baker. The roads are flanked at this time of year with sunflowers turning their smiling faces slowly as the day proceeds. Arriving back at La Merci Dieu, the grandfather and his son have arrived to complete the family get-together. More conversation, and then lunch followed by rest. My brother jokes that we only need a few more kids to complete a soccer team.

Late at night, Cécile's nine-year-old daughter Camille arrives. She has just spent time at girl scout camp and is distraught that she should now depart with us back to my brother Christian's house in Dortmund, but a soft teddy bear wins the argument. It is now almost midnight, as we start the long drive back through the night. I have never seen a moon as I have this night, big, bright, and orange, floating over the shadows of the stone houses and the sleeping fields. *Au revoir*, La Merci Dieu.

I took a small weekend trip to visit my friends in Portland, Oregon. It's a nice short hop from Oakland, barely long enough to digest the airline morsels. The pilot, or maybe the navigator (I couldn't tell which, does one count the stripes?), tells me, "It's only a buck to come in here," when he sees me glancing through the cockpit door with curiosity on the way to find my seat. A flight attendant proceeds to assure me that he is merely enhancing his retirement benefits. The trip is off to a good start. Alaska Airlines is one of the few airlines that still prides itself not only on good food but also customer service. The humor is reminiscent of the old PSA flight crews' humor. Take note, all you cattle-car airlines! Not that I shall mention any names.

After renting a car at PDX (I wonder how these abbreviated airport names came about, especially funny ones like LAX which sounds like something from a drugstore), I arrive at my friends' place in Beaverton, just outside of Portland. It is a wonderful reunion after three years. We chat quite a bit, and then Patrick goes off to open his restaurant. Da Vinci's, which is in Milwaukie, a small town outside of Portland along the Willamette River, is a culinary gem. Patrick learned his craft in San Francisco and now graces Portland with it. I hope some of you readers get a chance to stop by; the multitude of veal dishes alone would make the trip worthwhile. * My plan is to meet up with Sanae and Patrick at the restaurant later, so I take off in my little red rental car to go up the Columbia River, a locale I visited many years ago and that I want to photograph for the cookbook I'm writing.

I have never seen Oregon in the spring before, and I am amazed. After the wet spring in California with its usual profusion of wildflowers that are always a joy to behold, I am dumbstruck at seeing Oregon. It's so green, words can't do it justice. The day is a bit on the chilly side as I make my way along the Columbia River towards the Bonneville Dam. Small cascades of raindrops fall sporadically. The sky is a muddled gray and hundreds of birch trees with their bright black-and-white bark line the banks of the river, announcing spring with their sprouting new leaves, the majestic Columbia silently acknowledging them.

I arrive at the dam, park the car and walk toward the Visitor Center. The wind is trying its best to argue with my forward progress, but I duck that argument. My last visit here was roughly a baker's dozen years ago, although it was summer that time. At the lowest part of the Visitor Center building alongside several other exhibits are the "fish windows" where you can watch the fish swim by. It used to be that the salmon swimming upstream to spawn had to pass by the dam by jumping up the fish ladders built for them. The job has been made easier for them these days by holes that have been drilled in the various steps of the ladder, thus eliminating the jumping, but it's still a burden for them to make their way through the strong currents. It can take them upwards of 24 hours, depending on the species. Bonneville Dam employs several people in shifts to count and log the different species of salmon, which takes a keen eye and patience. Watching and waiting is rewarded with five salmon today.

After briefly stopping by the fish hatchery a short distance away, I make my way back toward Portland, taking the old highway through the mountains. It winds along the river and passes several breathtaking waterfalls. At one point, there is a plateau overlooking the vast river. The grandeur of creation lets one fall silent with awe. The wind and rain have really picked up now, as I make a stop by a small stand along the road and take a few pictures of brightly painted carved totem poles. Inside the stand, the smell of a wood stove and smoke greet the visitor. I buy some smoked salmon as has been requested of me back in

Oakland by friends, and after soaking up the warmth and a bit of the aroma and ambience of this little roadside stop, I depart.

I arrive back in Portland and walk through the streets a bit. On Saturdays, it has the feel of a small town, quiet and relaxed. People are enjoying their strolls and walks along the riverfront, and a few kids are playing soccer. Pink dogwoods with their big blossoms crowd the streets. Spring comes much later up here than in California. It is getting dark, time to navigate toward da Vinci's. Sanae seats me in the back and I get to sample Patrick's cuisine again. At the table next to me are a few kids on their prom dinner dates. It is really fun to watch them practicing to be young ladies and gentlemen. After a sumptuous meal I make my way back to see Patrick in the kitchen, trying not to get in the way this time. He is surprised that he has fed me already; lucky for me he didn't know that I was out there, otherwise I might not have been able to finish the meal, being told of larger portions he had in store for me. Glancing around the kitchen, it seems that the stoves have even more burners than the last time I was here. I don't know how Patrick does it, cooking all those lunches and dinners every day all by himself. Recently, cooking a special pancake breakfast for 50 to 60 people at church was a challenge for me -- and he does it every day, twice a day.

The following morning Sanae talks us into going out for brunch in downtown Portland. In front of the restaurant, a cherry tree whispers its blossoms on us, almost like snow. Sanae tells me how much the Japanese love this first sign of spring, and it's easy to understand why. Inside the restaurant I taste pear sherbet for the first time, and it is probably the finest sherbet I have ever eaten. Afterwards we visit the Japanese Garden with its abundance of blooming azaleas and hungry, active koi awakening from their winter slumber. The Forestry Center, our next stop nearby, showcases the evergreen history of

Oregon. At the entrance we are greeted by a multilingual tree talking up a storm about its various parts, and yes, I do make it talk in German by pressing the right button. The rest of Sunday and Monday fly by all too fast, and California calls me back via Charly the Eskimo.

* Author's note; Patrick has retired since I wrote this story; I'm sorry If I made you hungry.

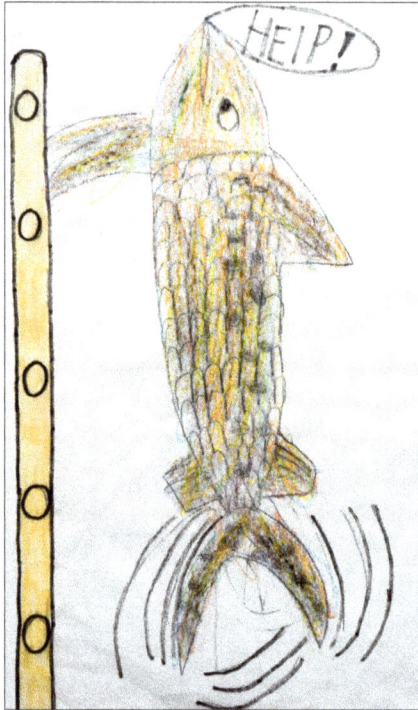

The Christmas Tree
Christmas 1998

I received plenty of bemused looks today for the following reason: crisscrossing the streets of San Francisco hunting for fares in my taxi, I'd spotted Christmas trees on outer Bush Street (a rather appropriate botanically named location, come to think of it). Cash and carry, seven and a half feet tall, I manage to fit him (and I'm jumping to conclusions here on the gender of my tree) into the trunk of my taxi, with perhaps two to three feet of branches sprouting out the back. Since my shift ends at 5:30, and the nursery closes at 2:00, I have little choice in the matter if I want a tree. My plan is to bring him to the cab garage for safekeeping until I can take him home in my truck after work.

When I have driven only a few blocks down Bush street, a waving hand catches my eye, and rather than obeying common sense and prior plans, my taxi instinct takes hold of me, so I pull over and pick up, with destination

Montgomery Street BART Station. My customer comments, "I didn't know taxis deliver trees now," so I have to explain to her that it's my tree. Going up and down the hills of San Francisco, the trunk flaps up and down on my poor, at this point probably very disgruntled, tree.

Here we are: BART. Bye! I hear a voice as my customer exits, "Can you take me to Bernal Heights, please?" But, but, but... "Oh, all right." All the way across town again. I get many looks from pedestrians: perhaps concerns of tree-napping. "That will be $10.20." "Thank you, merry Christmas!" Now to the garage. Oops, I hear a radio order, a possible pick-up not too far away for an airport trip, which is like waving bacon in front of a dog, and I respond to the dispatcher. I pull up, and two people emerge from the front of a building: "SFO, United Airlines please," one of them says, shedding curious glances at my tree and then me. "Oh, don't mind him," I respond, putting their luggage in the front seat.

So my now well-traveled evergreen, still a friend at this point, I hope, enjoys a tremendous clear view of the Bay and a quick trip to SFO. Here we are, thank you gentlemen. Finally it's back to the garage.

I promise you, O noble fir, tomorrow you will glow and shine!

Shaded Sands
April 1999

My friend Tom ran into a bit of a problem with the expiration of his driver's license as well as an expired Colorado registration for his truck. He was pondering his options of getting said truck back to Arizona without reaping the ire of the California Highway Patrol who appear on the long stretches of highway. I decided to offer him my help in driving his truck back, with the added benefit of companionship, and with any kind of luck, material for a new short story.

Departure time from Castro Valley: high noon on an April Friday. After brief instruction on Tom's part in the operation of his Chevy stick-shift, an antique from the 50s that he inherited from a relative, and then a gas and coffee fill-up, we start our trip over the Altamont Pass towards I-5. I am always amused at the propellers sans airplanes gracing the hills there. Realists would describe them as electricity-generating wind-turbines, or in similar terms.

The sound of the radio is drowned out when the speedometer of the old truck reaches its maximum, which is just about the highway's speed limit too, so we talk a bit instead, about our lives, loves, and children, as the long straightaway gathers dust behind us. Tom has spent many miles on the road as a traveling craftsman, and is familiar with the highways. Whereas he could probably tell you just about each and every number of every highway on our way to Arizona, I remember the more important items such as the billboard advertising fresh delicious peach pie. We make several stops for gas, and it seems the old truck is satisfied with no less than twenty dollars' worth every time. As late afternoon approaches, we climb over the "Grapevine," which gives view to the Los Angeles Basin. The California Aqueduct which had crossed our path along I-5 a few times along the way now makes its way up the hill, the water in the enormous pipes defying gravity. Oh, I almost forgot to mention: the radio at this point in time, barely audible over the engine noise, sweetly surrounds us with the sound of Beethoven from a radio station in Bakersfield (which should lay to rest a few generalizations about country and culture).

We turn east on Highway 138, one of the very few roads Tom has not been on. After numerous requests on my part to stop at the peach pie restaurant that the aforementioned billboard advertised, and which Tom refuses to agree to because of some rather bad memories concerning his overindulgence in dried peaches, we then compromise and settle for dinner at a Bakers Square restaurant in the town with the southern-California-sounding name of Palmdale. An unexpected very chilly wind gusts over the high terrain, seeming to belie the presence of palms around us. As we leave the restaurant, I receive a funny look from the waitress when I ask if I can take along some of their crayons with me. Must be my Tom Sawyer instinct taking over.

It is now approaching dusk. We head further east on 138 through the high desert and are greeted by the first Joshua trees (or *yucca brevifolia*, for those of you botanically inclined) scattered in the barren landscape. Rather surprisingly, they are part of the lily family, and bloom white in the summer. They were named by the Mormons in the 1850s because the trees reminded them of Joshua's arms leading them to the promised land. With a dark blue sky as backdrop and then the dark orange glow of the setting sun, we take a few snapshots in this pristine wilderness before returning to the pleasant heat of the truck, as the night has turned cold now. Again, a misconception of the desert as being only a hot place is disproved. We make our way past Apple Valley, a strange sounding name for a place in the desert -- or perhaps they were thinking of dessert when naming it? Our intention is to spend the night close to Joshua Tree National Monument, which we hope to visit in the early morning. From the standpoint of the average tourist, we probably could have figured out that searching for a motel at night without a reservation, with April being the prime time for visiting the desert, was, shall we say, not particularly bright on our part. Finally a "Vacancy" sign announcing our rest stop for the night comes into view, after driving along the endless road of "No Vacancy" signs. We are exhausted from the drive, but nonetheless decide to set the alarm to get up early the next day, so as not to miss the beautiful light of early morning.

As I stumble into the shower the next morning, I ponder that although from a historical perspective it seems highly unlikely that Napoleon has frequented the Desert Sky Motel & R.V. Park, it nonetheless appears a distinct possibility, judging by the placement of the shower head, which dispenses water just slightly above my belly button.

We check out and navigate towards coffee. After finding some and climbing back into the truck, I notice Tom's cup has no lid. He tells me he couldn't find one. I go back inside the store and after asking, find one. The cashier remarks, "We hide them so people will talk to us."

Smokey the Bear greets us and alerts us to low fire danger as we enter the north side of Joshua Tree National Monument. The sun has risen quicker than we have, but the morning chill still hangs about us. As we drive down the entrance road, it becomes quite apparent that we have entered a national park, as the natural scenery asserts itself, devoid of litter and advertising. We come to a peak at the western end of one of the main roads and climb out to take the footpath the rest of the way to promises of a vantage point. The air is incredibly clear but ice cold, convincing us to put on sweatshirts and jackets. We gaze at the Palm Springs area below, the purple-hues of the mountains

Joshua Tree Nat'l. Monument

in the far distance. The cold, however, quickly sends us back to the confines of the truck. Driving east, the Joshua trees are still plentiful, and amazing granite rock formations suited to a moonscape surround us. It is as if a giant had played with rocks, balancing and stacking them for his amusement. The colors of these enormous boulders range in hue from light sand to adobe to orange to rust. They look so inviting that we stop to do some rock climbing. Looks can be deceiving, as the rocks which seemed smooth and round when viewed from a distance turn out to be quite "rough around the edges". As we duck through a tunnel and emerge onto a ledge, the truck appears matchbox-sized below us; however, it could be that my imagination is running away with me here a bit. The view from the plateau affords a look at the awakening desert. My hopes of encountering a road runner or its nemesis, the coyote, are not to be, however.

Back in the truck, we continue south, and the number of rock formations gradually diminishes as we make the transition to the low desert. The vast expanse that stretches before us now is ringed by low mountains on either side. Creosote bushes, teddy bear and chain-fruit cholla dot the landscape in a display of fierce survival. The creosote bushes are thought to be the oldest living things on earth. Our seasonal timing is impeccable: dozens of ocotillos, desert dwellers stretching their long thin arms heavenward, are in full bloom. Their bright orange-red flowers make a spectacular contrast to the cerulean sky. We walk, then stand in awe in the quiet morning desert silence. My shoe comes too close to a cholla at one point, and the hooked spines implant themselves immediately, demonstrating the plant's instantaneous natural defense system. Thank God it was too early in the day for flip-flops.

The tail-end of our visit to the park comes all too soon. Highway 10, the long straight desert road to Arizona, greets us. The sun is high in the sky now, but the temperature a pleasant spring one. Our stomachs grumble for breakfast. We pull over at the Desert Center Cafe, just a short stretch off the main highway. There is a curious circle of date palms nearby, I suspect the doings of a man trying to establish an oasis. A fenced-in area displays a collector's mecca of gold mining utensils and old machinery. A pleasant Hispanic girl serves us breakfast, and in hindsight, I should have ordered the date milk shake, despite the menu's insistence on its being a better companion with lunch. The local paper on the counter has an amazing statistic: the night before, the temperature at Tejon Pass near the Grapevine had been 23° F, which was colder than any other temperature in the U.S., including Alaska, for that night.

Well nourished, we continue. We cross the Arizona border at the great Colorado River and stop again to provide for the thirsty old Chevy, with its endless appetite for fuel. Entering this new state, the change in scenery is immediate. I see the first saguaro cacti of my life, hunkering like giant one- or two-armed bandits on the red rock desert slopes. Tom assures me there are saguaro from here to the end of Arizona, slowing my impulse to stop to capture them on film right away. As we roll along Highway 10, Tom, who has somehow talked me into letting him drive, stays right behind a heavily loaded truck that is taking full advantage of Arizona's higher speed limit, ignoring the distinction the speed limit signs make between speeds for cars and trucks. This practice is known as "slipstreaming," or in other words, riding in the truck's wind shadow to conserve fuel. I'm not surprised the truck drivers frown upon this, as they are unable to see you in their mirrors.

As the Arizona desert floats by us, I can see the illusion of water in the road ahead in the noonday sun, as so often happens in these parts. However, I ignore the recommendation for a swim the driver makes to his shotgun-riding partner. I marvel at the similarity of what is depicted on the Arizona license plate and what meets the eye along this long stretch of blacktop. Not only the scattered saguaro everywhere, but the maroons and purples of the mountain ranges are the image of the scenic plate. I convince Tom to deviate from our originally planned "as-the-crow-flies" route, to take a detour to see a site that I have located while perusing the map -- Organ Pipe Cactus National Monument -- so we turn south on Highway 85. Towns along the way with names such as Gila Bend and Ajo conjure up images of what one thinks of as the Southwest.

I finally do find a road runner -- he decorates an auto repair facility in the form of a large sign. We come through a town called Why; in the center of this quiet border town is a beautiful whitewashed adobe church. Why? Why not? Had to make that pun, didn't you? A road sign now advises us to turn our radio to a set frequency which then produces the voice of a park ranger welcoming us to and explaining the highlights of Organ Pipe Cactus National Monument. The long, straight, remote stretch of road in this Sonoran Desert is bordered by hundreds and hundreds of saguaro and organ pipe cacti, the latter being immigrants from Mexico. The late afternoon plays with their long shadows and the sky is a deep dark Ektachrome blue. It's a miracle that anything can survive in this harsh, unmerciful climate of extremes. A brochure speaks of ground temperatures reaching 175 °F in the heat of summer, an unimaginable scorching heat. We toy with the idea of crossing the border into Mexico since we are so close, but common sense prevails; we'll save it for another trip. I tend to think the Mexican authorities would probably object to Tom's expired registration tags and license.

After another fill-up, we head through an Indian reservation towards Tucson -- we still have some miles to tread. Texas longhorns, seemingly well aware of their free range status, greet us occasionally. I don't know why, but this stretch of road has many white crosses along it, a grim reminder of highway safety. Night engulfs us as we reach the outskirts of Tucson. We find Highway 10 again and stop for dinner at the TTT truck stop. Tom tells me not to look too conspicuous as we enter the "trucker only" section of the dining room, having parked the little old Chevy outside next to the dozens of resting behemoths awaiting their captains' return to continue their cross country journeys. I guess I might look a little out of place, with my cameras, but I think the drivers we talk to enjoy a little chit-chat and are hardly concerned with our presence despite no proof of a big rig. The topic of the night is the disparity in gas prices between Arizona and California, or as Tom corrects me, fuel, not gas, which is what truckers call it. Pardon me, but after all, I am traveling in an itty-bitty old Chevy. The most interesting sight to me in here is that next to each table is a telephone, which as I think further about this, of course makes sense, since freight and transit require communications. After some good cheeseburgers, we leave to make the final segment to Tom's folks' house. We stumble into Hereford and get a warm welcome. We are beat, after having traveled well over 1200 miles in two days.

The next morning brings our surroundings into daylight. This southeastern part of Arizona lies at an altitude of around 4000 feet, and snow sometimes graces the top of a nearby rugged mountain range. Tom's dad tells me the climate is temperate here, even in the summer, because of the altitude (unlike the desert stretches that we had encountered prior). As I look around, I notice an unfamiliar contraption sitting on the roof of a house in the distance, and upon further observation, also on the one I'm sitting in. The shape is that of a chimney, but it is something quite different: it is an evaporater cooler, commonly known as a "swamp cooler." It works by sucking in fresh air from the outside through cooling pads into the aluminum ducts. Water is fed via drip lines to the pads (which consist of shredded pine or aspen fibers), and the air is cooled as it passes through the pads. An ingenious invention. It turns out that the pads are due to be replaced, so we pay the roof a visit and put theory into practice amidst a gusting wind. Gotta take advantage of those young workers.

The following day Tom takes me to the town of Tombstone. As we enter the town, the charm of the old west is immediately on view: white picket fences in front of many of the houses, wooden sidewalks that are often covered, stagecoaches, and old brick buildings. A gunsmith proudly advertises his business under a flowing red, gold and blue Arizona State flag. Inside the store, dozens of Winchester rifles glisten on the shelves. In neighboring shops, cowboy hats, boots and belts exude the sweet smell of leather. Above the O.K. Corral hangs the sign "Walk where they fell," a grim reminder of the rougher frontier days here. Cochise County's history boasts names such as Geronimo, Wyatt Earp, and Frederick Remington. Although the gunfights are now only simulated, the mystique of a bygone era undeniably hangs above Tombstone. People "vacation" here working on cattle ranches. The authenticity of hard physical work seems to act as a magnet for cubicle-dwelling city residents, whereas I'm sure some locals would trade the Wild West for modern creature comforts.

We continue south to Bisbee, a town nestled in a canyon, and the site of the huge former Copper Queen Mine. Craft stores and old hotels line the main street. We park and walk down the main street of this town that has become home to artists and craftsmen. A funny sight in one of the parking spaces: a new Volkswagen Beetle painted in soccer ball colors and design. Tom says: "Makes you wanna kick it." We enter an establishment promising and then holding true to its promise of an ice cold beer. It turns out that this bar was formerly the only stock exchange west of the Mississippi in the copper mine days. Blackboards from floor to ceiling still display faded stock market quote chalk marks. Who would have guessed! On one of the side streets, we encounter an old "Strayhound," a slightly renamed Greyhound bus most likely belonging to an old hippie from the Sixties. An Indian motorcycle advertisement complements the scene.

My last day in Arizona comes all too quickly. I teach Tom the final details of e-mail use on a Macintosh I have given him so we can keep in touch. I like his choice of e-mail name, "Shaded Sands". It is time for me to depart, and we head to Tucson Airport. On the outskirts of Tucson is an amazing sight: hundreds and hundreds of mothballed airplanes sit in the desert, waiting for someone to awaken their roaring engines once again. The dry air prevents them from rusting. They seem so out of place here. Saguaro cacti decorate even the airport terminals as we pull up in front of Southwest. I hate good-byes, so "until next time". As the plane climbs to its comfortable altitude, I ponder the rich sights of the past few days. The seat row I am in is very unusual, arranged in train-like fashion with the seats facing each other. As the silver bird begins its ascent, the flight attendant has a joke for us: "Did you hear about the peanut that went to New York City?" "He was a salted."

Impressions of France
Summer 1999

The early-morning summer skies of Paris embrace the big bird as it starts its descent. Fields in hues of green and gold pastels can be seen clearly through my small porthole. Soon the vast metropolis unfolds below. The flight attendants prepare the cabin for arrival. Sleepy-eyed passengers stretch, blink, and wake up with anticipation. As the reverse thrust of the engines on the ground slows us to taxi speed, carriers from different countries delight the eye at their resting places next to us. The cabin doors open, the shuffling of feet and clicking of overhead bins increases. We are here. As I make my way to customs, I shake off California and step on French soil (or concrete, as the case may be). I proceed down a long corridor to the line for EU nationals. *"Bonjour, Monsieur."* "You are lucky," the officer greets me as he checks my passport and waves me through. I smile back and am eager to step outside for much-awaited fresh air. A very pretty French policewoman directs me to the Air France bus.

I am on my way to pick up my Renault Twingo but have to travel from Orly to Charles de Gaulle to do so. Oh, those little last-minute mix-ups in airports, but I don't care, I'm here, and I get a sparrow perspective high up as the bus traverses Paris for 50 minutes. The bus is flanked by an armada of small cars scooting by, left and right, on the early morning commute. On the video monitor, a pleasant tourist information guide and his sidekick, an animated and cheerful French bus, proceed to give us instructions about the airports and other pertinent traveler information. I gaze out the window, absorbing the new sights. The sun starts its morning climb as the bus pulls into the terminal at CDG. I pass through a hallway and talk on a telephone, whose voice soon appears in a live version to pick me up to claim my car. After brief formalities, I find my Twingo, "La Bleu" I name her, slumbering in a

Claye - Souilly - France

corner all by herself. After satisfying her thirst with *sans plomb 95*, I navigate toward the *Autoroute* with destination Reims, a halfway point between Germany and France recommended by my brother as a place to spend the night.

The beauty of the intense bright red poppies sticking their heads out between the long stalks of golden wheat fields along the *Autoroute* greets me, but soon jet lag begins to take effect, and my eyes start to argue for sleep. I exit at the *péage* booth, mumbling another "*Bonjour,*" and continue straight into Reims. As I make my way along the streets, a sign suggesting an inexpensive peaceful slumber at the Hotel d'Alsace beckons. I park and inquire with my seventh grade French about the price of the *chambre*: "*Avec petit dejeuner? Avec douche? Bon!"* The now boulder-containing suitcase somehow ascends the numerous small stairs with me, and after a shower, the necessity of counting sheep becomes a moot point.

The evening breeze coming through the window wakes me, and after inquiring downstairs of the innkeeper what time breakfast starts, I walk into Reims. Wow, I'm in France, it dawns on me as I shake off a year's work and tell my mind I'm on vacation. I look at the white and amber colored houses with their window shutters painted blue, red, and green, geraniums gracing their planter boxes, their attic windows protruding near the rooftops.

People are strolling in the warm summer night. I pass by a fish-monger's shop whose doors are now closed, but I make a mental note of it for the morning. I walk past several restaurants and what appear to be ancient Roman ruins, then stroll back to the restaurants and am invited by the menu of Brasserie du Boulingrin. I sit at a table outside, soaking it all up. *"Bonsoir, Monsieur,"* the waiter smiles, giving me a menu. I am able to identify salmon, *les escargots*, and asparagus.

Oh, what a blessing to sit for three hours and dine at leisure watching the sky turn a dark India ink, the street lamps doing their nighttime duty, as the hum of soft words, a few prowling bats, and happy evening pedestrians surround me. The German expression of "living like God in France" dances in my head.

Croissants, bread, honey, and a *café au lait* grace the breakfast table as I see a few other early birds beside me come into the small dining room. It is so nice to hear the *"Bonjours"* as people enter. The small pleasantries in life. I intend to visit the fishmonger, and before doing so must locate an ice chest. I ask the innkeeper if there is a supermarket nearby. She draws me a map and I nod politely. A guest standing next to me guesses right that I didn't understand a word, taps me on the shoulder and motions me to follow him. I walk down the street with him and he takes me to his car and drives me all the way to an open *supermarché*. How kind! I thank him and shop for some French specialties to bring to my family. The ice chest eludes me at this store, however. I lock the items into La Bleu and walk into *centreville*. The magnificent Gothic cathedral of Reims, with its gargoyles and the famous smiling angel, greets me. A group of French schoolchildren are singing at one end of the cathedral where the beautiful blue stained glass windows by Marc Chagall are glowing, iridescent. I cannot help but sit quietly for a while to look and listen. I think to myself about showing this to my sons when I pick them up in a week.

I walk to a bank nearby, and after a failed attempt outside at exchanging currency with a rather uncooperative machine, I am assisted inside by a helpful human teller. Here I also find success with my impending purchase of the ice chest. I draw a picture of an igloo and ice cubes and learn that I am looking for an *isotherme*. A few landmarks are pointed out to me in the direction of the department store I need to go to. *Merci!* Armed with my *isotherme,* I head for the fishmonger, and purchase *crevettes* (shrimp with their cute little heads still on) to bring to my brother, sister-in-law and goddaughter as a treat. The smiling fishmonger gives me some ice for my *isotherme*. After a visit to the *patisserie,* a few loaves of heavenly-smelling bread and *croissants* richer, I twingo myself back to the *Autoroute*.

The fields pass by as I drive in the noonday laziness. Suddenly I glance next to me as a herd of Coca-Cola-advertisement-adorned "Smarts," a new electric vehicle unknown to me and half the size of my tiny car, goes by. I'm dumbstruck by their size, quietness, and speed. They don't quite fit my picture of France. I can't help but smile at one of the drivers of these matchbox cars. He grins back and zips by.

The Lorraine region falls behind me and Saarbrücken approaches. I am in my country. La Bleu now enjoys a little *bleifrei* gas, and after purchase of a phone card, I call my brother and tell him arrival will be in the evening. It's been a while since I have driven on an *Autobahn*, and I pass the slow trucks with caution as the speed demons race by me. In the early evening I come to Marburg, my brother's new home town. As I glance up at the castle sitting on the mountainside of this small town on the Lahn river, I come to a phone booth. I try to describe to my brother where I am. "Oh, you are about two blocks away," he tells me.

Anne and my goddaughter Natascha greet me. I don't know how, but Natascha discovers the candy in the side pocket of my car immediately. Kids must have a homing instinct for sweets. The *crevettes* have held up well, and follow me to their ultimate destiny in the kitchen: shrimp scampi.

A week later, I pick up my offspring after navigating through the maze of Charles de Gaulle. As I see them come through Immigration I can't help but notice a disparity between my prior advice of packing light and what I see. Luckily, my stuff already resides in Germany, so La Bleu can gobble up what remains. We depart and stop in the city of Meaux for the boys' first French breakfast, although Coke and OJ might not exactly fit that bill. We then visit several small shops; Patrick later tells me that one of the shopkeepers complimented him on his French. The position of navigator is established as Christian dispenses route information from the road atlas with the waving Michelin Man on the cover, as we drive along the country roads next to the Marne River. I'm so excited about getting off the main *Autoroute* and seeing the real France that I forget my sons just got off a plane, and are probably getting jet lag. We have a picnic along the Marne about halfway to Reims (as I recall I was short-changed on either the cheese or the tomatoes). We arrive in Reims, and the suggestion of a hotel with a bathtub is made, as I shall phrase it here with diplomacy. After inquiring at a few places, we find Hotel Le Champagne. We ascend the curving staircases until we find our rooms under the roof-top. I glance out at the promenade of trees below us. We agree to meet up after a nap. Later, I take Patrick to the same restaurant I'd found a week before, while his brother is still out like a rock (an expression that has always been thought-provoking to me). I enjoy watching as Patrick deciphers the menu and the waitress is kind enough to bring us some extra bread for Christian. We stroll back through the evening streets of Reims enjoying the last rays of sun.

In the morning after breakfast, I show the boys the magnificent cathedral. After we check out of our hotel, we pick up a few *baguettes,* which then sit in the back window of La Bleu as we continue through the countryside of the Champagne region, despite my sons' protests about not using the *Autoroute* instead, and occasional navigation glitches.

The vineyards sprawl on the soft earthy hills in the warm noonday sun. Beautiful red rose bushes are planted at the front of each row of grapes. At this time of day the towns of white stone houses with red tile roofs lie in quiet and peaceful slumber, their summer way of life. We stop and visit one of the few *champagne* houses that is open. Beautiful glassware and tradition are on display here. Afterward, we drive along the kind of road flanked on both sides by endless rows of trees that is common in France, reminders of a past when shade was a necessity for walking here in the hot summers. I'm finally talked into the *Autoroute*, as Christian & Patrick are anxious to see their grand-parents in Ilmesmühle.

Jumping ahead a few weeks: our last day in Germany approaches, and it's time to say goodbye, which is always the hardest part of visiting. We bid my parents goodbye. One of the St. Bernards isn't feeling well and the other one is still sleepy this morning, so they have to miss their customary last walk with me. Having cleaned La Bleu at a car wash the day before in preparation for departure, my luck in attracting rain just after washing vehicles continues, this time in the form of a thundershower. Well, at least the inside of the car has stayed clean. One last wave from the window, and we head off towards France, completely surrounded by luggage this time. Don't know how we fit it all.

We cross the border and travel on the *Autoroute* towards Paris. I pull off in Verdun to find a bank for the last currency conversion. A pity we don't have time left to see this city. We get back on the A4 and this time we parallel some of last time's scenic routes along the Marne. As the evening approaches we reach the outskirts of Paris. We drive through a village by the name of Messy (probably named after a kid's room) looking for a place for the night, then head back to the secondary road alongside fields of parading sunflowers glorifying summer. We stop in the town of Claye-Souilly, a hop skip and jump from CDG, and find a perfect accommodation, two rooms -- one for *les enfants*, one *pour moi,* connected by a hallway. I am amazed at Patrick's ability to converse with the innkeeper after his two years of French. As the warm evening turns to dusk we walk down the street for one last French meal. A kid on the street sees that Patrick is from the US, and coaxes a demo of spinning a basketball on his finger out of him. We find a place that specializes in *crêpes*, two of which are *flambéd* at our table, always a sight to behold. As we walk back to our hotel, myself slightly inebriated (or so I'm told), I have to think of van Gogh's night sky painting.

Dawn finds us soon, and we pack and head off towards CDG. By instinct I find the right terminal again and drop off my boys. See you in the US; behave yourselves! I now have four hours before my flight departs from Orly. I'm determined to visit La Défense, an architectural marvel I have seen in a guidebook. After several detours which result from taking the map as a suggestion rather than a guide, I find parking under this super-enormous structure. As I take the elevator upstairs, the faint glow of the rising sun greets me under a blanket of gray. I'm dumbstruck at the scale of the urban plateau before me: a vast stretch of stone walkways interspersed with fountains, shallow pools of water, sculptures, and behemoth office towers of glass and concrete. What a sight! Modern pioneers have fulfilled their building dreams. I walk to one end of La Défense and see the Tour Eiffel and Arc de Triomphe in the distance, a juxtaposition to this vast modern expanse. Putting things in perspective, a black cat casually strolls by. An early morning worker is silhouetted against the sky as he cleans the ponds of debris. I walk from one end of La Défense to the other trying to capture some of this spectacle on film.

After my last *café au lait* with *croissant* crumbs for the quick sparrows underneath the tables and chairs, I head back downstairs to find and return La Bleu. On the road, I get lost again and am offered a little help at a BP station somewhere on the outskirts of Paris. I find the *Périphérique* and throw myself into the morning commute. I see a taxi and yell out the window: *"Pardon Monsieur,* Orly?" Oh, it's frustrating not to be able to speak in complete sentences, but he yells back something with *"sud"* in it, all at a speed of perhaps 50-60 kilometers per hour. *"Merci,"* brother! Sure enough, Orly comes into sight and the sadness at giving back La Bleu becomes inevitable. It's true: once you drive a Twingo, you will never want to give it back! At the check-in counter a sign greets me: one piece of carry-on luggage only. Oh-oh, different rules here than at SFO. An adorable employee of American Airlines smiles at my question, is it OK to have two pieces: "No, it's not OK, but I let you." *Merci, Mademoiselle*! A bus takes us to our airplane on the runway, something I haven't experienced since I was a kid. The thrust of the engines propels us away from a now-awake Paris.

À bientot!

In Goethe's Footsteps
Summer 1999

The alarm rings, demanding "rise and shine". As I look out the meadow window of the barn, a hint of morning dew is visible on the field. We have a big day ahead. I pass the beds of the two comatose and tiptoe into the shower, trying to avoid a later comparison with heavy footed lumbering animals.

The leaves of the *Linde* rustle slightly in the wind as I walk quietly across to the mill and open the glass door. The two St. Bernards are still snoozing as I make my way to the kitchen. I have been detected, however, as Mauke's tail whaps with joy on the wooden floor. I go over to pet her and she whines like a baby, a habit solely hers. Merlot, the seemingly more sensible one, is still asleep.

Several scoops later, followed by the bubbling of hot water, the strong smell of coffee fills the early morning hour. I walk back outside with the hedgehog coffee cup and sit on the steps in front of the glass door, inhaling the fresh air that's already starting to warm up. A few epiphyllums are attempting to greet the day as birds parade around the cobblestones.

Another wake-up call is due for Christian and Patrick. Mission accomplished, they find the shower. I retreat back to the kitchen and start preparing some hearty *Käse* and *Schinken* sandwiches for lunch. On the agenda is a trip to Weimar, which has the proud distinction of being the cultural city of Europe for 1999, an open invitation for a visit. The plan for the day is for each of us to walk in different directions once we get there, and to see what photos we can come up with -- a delightful suggestion from my brother Holger.

When we're packed and ready, the gravel road takes us past the Ilmesmühle entrance stone and down to the B27. Left behind, the St. Bernards are happy to have regained their peace. In Bad Hersfeld the *Autobahn*, already congested with trucks, leads to now unfamiliar territory in the former East Germany. After an extended stretch of hills and forests, we come into the flatter region of Thüringen. As we exit and come to the outskirts of Weimar, a large parking lot beckons visitors to leave their cars and stroll to the pedestrian-friendly points. We split up to begin our day's adventure.

Entering the historic city, it is evident how hard the people have been at work to restore it. Residences, museums, and stores have been painted in aesthetic shades of earth tone pastels, with red and dark gray slate and shingle roofs to complement them. As I stroll through a park, majestic old oaks surrounding me, a few students bicycle past. A slight sheet of rain falls, and I duck for shelter under one of the much-praised and cherished trees of German literature. As the drops subside, I emerge onto a main street that leads to an open square. Symmetrical short, round trees flank one side of a long building, and a statue of Goethe riding a horse is visible in the center.

Encountering a few American tourists, I chat briefly with them. They are absolutely thrilled to be here and to discover the Weimar which they have only known from history books. Around the corner, past a few famous hotels, I stop to pet one of the two horses that are patiently standing and dozing near the curb, awaiting another call to duty to once again slowly pull the cart of eager visitors around this city of writers and poets.

Goethe has been immortalized here, everywhere: on cafe signs, books, posters, lamp posts. I watch a few workmen laying cobblestones and see a banner hanging above them, proclaiming "Look towards

Landstraße in Thüringen

the heavens, O human". I wonder what Goethe would think of this modern era.

As I search for a bookstore, the emblem of the city -- a black lion on yellow background, adorning a bright red fire truck -- pops into view on a side street. Around the corner a six-foot-tall nutcracker greets me. Inside the store his smaller brothers and sisters patiently await children's eyes and hands, jaws eager to crunch the nuts the squirrels failed to find. Lunch consists of an excellent local beer and *Schmalzbrot*, as Schiller and Goethe watch from their statuesque presence in the square. After purchasing several of Goethe's works in one of the many bookstores that Weimar boasts, I head toward the meeting point at the entrance to the park, under the chestnut trees.

We exchange some of our impressions of the day. Since it is still early afternoon, Christian mentions we should stop by Jena, a city famous for its hand-blown glass and quite nearby, according to our map.

Jena, at first glance, is more of an industrial city, and the differences between it and Weimar are quite stark: it is still in need of the loving touch of paint. One of the showrooms of the famous Jena glass factories is still open, and on display are exquisite translucent pieces of form and color.

Leaving the city, we cross a bridge over the river Saale. After about an hour or so of mostly sitting in traffic, we decide to get off the *Autobahn* for dinner. The trip through the countryside is reward-ing: fields of flowing golden wheat as far as the eye can see, with delicate blue, purple, and white wildflowers bordering them. As in France, rows of trees flank the road; this time, however, the trees are short and more widely dispersed. Gotha becomes our dinner stop. The small inexpensive menu has some local specialties and *soljanka,* a soup of Russian origin -- a reminder that not so long ago this was still East Germany. After dinner, Patrick decides to stay in the car. I take a walk with Christian through a park, past some restored brick buildings which give the impression they might have been a train roundhouse at one time. My impeccable homing instinct for Italian ice cream finds a store behind one of the brick buildings. Tasting of white wine and grapes, it is the best ice cream I have ever eaten, even better than the sherbet in Portland.

As nightfall quickly comes, we leave Gotha behind, and the roads are now populated with only a few cars here and there. Thunder can be heard in the distance, and a downpour of flood proportions ensues. The wiper fights a valiant battle as we travel along slowly. Lightning bolts flash across the night sky, etching out curtains of purple and blue. We are now alongside the mountainous terrain of the Wartburg made famous by Martin Luther. Its illuminated walls rise out of the ground from its mountaintop perch, as lightning strikes again. If not for sitting in a car, one would expect knights to appear at any moment, charging down the hill.

As the rain lets up somewhat, trucks crawl slowly up the last hills entering the state of Hessen. A cracked window lets in the sweet smell of the night air. We are almost home. The *Linde* greets us again, and at the glass door two brown and white faces appear, tails wagging with anticipation.

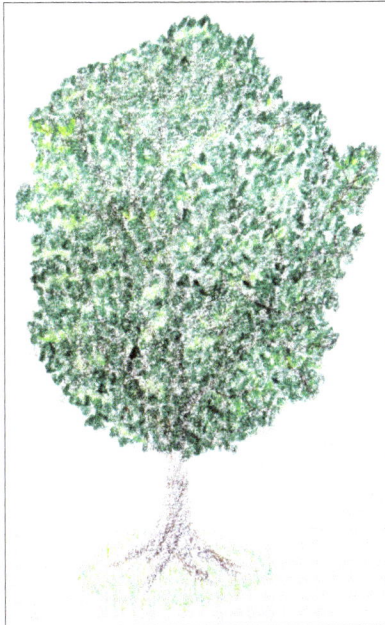

Carmel Valley, California

Fish Camping
August 1999

The waning days of summer brought an overnight trip to the Monterey Peninsula, a gemstone of California one never needs an excuse to visit. A customer had informed me about a special event at the Monterey Bay Aquarium, thus encouraging me to really pay closer attention in the future to my member newsletter that comes in the mail. The article in question proclaimed that several times during the summer, members can spend a night camping at the aquarium. I was hooked, if you'll pardon the expression.

It's a foggy Saturday morning as I pack my sleeping bag, culture bag (a literal translation of a German word for toiletry) and other weekend items and head out the door to my truck. Fueled by a hot cup of coffee, I leave my rented room in Castro Valley and navigate over the San Mateo bridge. The Bay shimmers, a flat, gray, endless mass, as the morning dew peels off the windshield in drops. Traffic is very sparse on the bridge in the direction of Half Moon Bay. Passing Santa's tree farm of bushy evergreens standing in tin soldier formation and at attention on the right side, I'm now close to scenic Highway 1.

Along the coast, as I pull over at one of my favorite pit stops, Big Basin, I spot dozens of windsurfers zipping along on the ocean's surface surrounded by whitecaps, the playful wind at their disposal. A few of the rather numerous sails are translucent, giving them the appearance of dragonfly wings. It is a dazzling, dancing spectacle I have to pry myself away from.

The artichoke fields of Castroville surround the highway on both sides. A final late-afternoon pit stop in Sand City sees the purchase of an air mattress. Armed with same, I make my final approach towards Cannery Row, entrusting my faithful old truck to a parking garage stall for the night.

I walk down the Row, which is starting to slide into nighttime slumber, to take in dinner at a local restaurant. Out of regard for our fine finned friends, I opt for the steak tonight. At a table next to mine, I observe a waiter as he elegantly spins a salad bowl, making it dance in place while slowly adding ingredients for a Caesar salad into it. The picture of a seal balancing a ball on its nose or a person spinning a basketball on the tip of a finger come to mind as I watch this very artful performance. The waiter relishes the customers' attention and awe.

It is dusk as I make my way back to the garage to gather my "fish camping" gear. I'm excited. Stuff protruding from under my arms left and right, I make my way down towards the Aquarium, as the night air engulfs the now silently sitting gray concrete building slabs.

Along with close to probably two hundred "campers" of all ages, I stow my stuff away, and then we make our way to the main auditorium, where we are greeted by cheerful volunteers. After explaining some of the ground rules for the night to us, they educate us not only about the complex ecosystem involving the otter, but also about marine kelp forests, harbor seals, and the present state of affairs of orcas found off the coast of Alaska. A young girl has the privilege of dressing up as an otter, adding fur components one by one as the guides continue with their explanations. From stage right an orca enters the scene and makes strides towards the unsuspecting otter, which at the last moment, sensing impending danger, delicately outmaneuvers the orca and ducks behind a volunteer. Laughter and applause!

The highlight of the evening comes a little later when we are allowed to feed the bat rays (a privilege normally reserved for their keepers) by holding shrimp out in a flat hand underneath them so their mouths can find them. They are like puppies nibbling at fingers and darting around excitedly. I have a feeling they know exactly when it is time to eat. Milk and cookies, now, for the two-legged mammals, provide an invitation to settle in for the night.

It is amusing to see all the sleeping bags rolled out and laid in front of the various exhibits, reminding me of comments by a friend: "I guess you'll be sleeping with the fishes," and "Who's watching who?" I find an appealing spot under the anchovies, a circular tank on the ceiling not unlike a cheese bell. Gazing upward, I follow them as they swim, sometimes racing as if fleeing a predator, sometimes moving sluggishly in endless circles, and I am lulled to sleep.

Dawn arrives, and my culture bag and I briefly descend the stairs to the rest rooms, before going outside and inhaling some fresh Pacific salt air on the outer decks of the aquarium, as the sun makes its ascent over the vast blue Monterey Bay.

The smell of hot oatmeal and coffee lures me back inside to my fellow campers. After a healthy breakfast, we are allowed one quick last round of the tanks before giving way to the workers starting their day of duties and preparations in expectation of the regular daily visitors.

Leaving the aquarium, I walk along Cannery Row past a long series of murals depicting a bygone Steinbeck era and then, crossing the street, see the seagulls' fight over the garbage cans awaiting morning pickup. I plan to attend service in Carmel Valley this morning, but first I head to

Carmel Beach, with its beautiful white sand, as there is still some time to spare before the service will begin. Quite a few dogs are running around exuberantly on this early Sunday morning. Oh, to be a dog in the town of Carmel -- what a privilege! The fog still hangs over the beach, turning sand and sky into one continuous color. The smell of the Monterey cypress trees drifts through the fog.

After service, I opt to take Los Laureles Grade over the golden hills to the coast highway, rather than going back through the valley again. Near Seaside, I do a double take as I spot a scuba diver in the sky. Upon further observation, he turns out to be a kite, along with what must be at least a hundred other kites in all colors and shapes filling the sky. I just have to pull over and take another walk along the beach to look at this spectacle. If anyone ask you if pigs can fly, yes, they can, or so the flying ice cream cone would tell you.

New Year's in Oregon
December 1999/January 2000

As La Niña made her entrance into California this winter, I had the privilege of going up to Portland for a long weekend. I booked my flight via the web, chasing the dangling carrot in the form of free airline miles, the reward for exploring this brand new method of booking a flight on Alaska Airlines. At the airport is another surprise: one can print out boarding passes on a touch screen. The pilot seems to be in a hurry -- we take off rather quickly. As the plane gains altitude, the outline of Alameda Island, with its rows and rows of blinking lights, appears through the fog. After a turn to the north, the view below us is of the bridges over the Bay, which are especially beautiful at night in this soft winter grayness. Later, as we land in Portland, the pilot announces that travelers with checked luggage will be able to retrieve same in two to three days.

I find my rental car patiently waiting for me, hiding in one of the many rows of cars. I have never before been to my first destination of this trip, S.E. Salmon Street. Relying on my instinct and navigation skills, I ignore the complimentary map received at the rental counter. Well, after driving in big circles twice and seeing the same landmarks again, with bug-like attraction Mr. "I don't need-directions" is lured by the neon lights of fast food, to ask the way. One taco later, I am on my way. Strangely enough, although I have never seen it, I pull up in front of my friends' house knowing that it is the right one. Long time no see! I follow them into the kitchen, always the best place in the house. Cuong and Jackie have turned it into one of the most charming ones I have ever seen, a cook's dream, with bright light and lots of space and warmth throughout. It is apparent to me that their roots are taking hold after three years up here in the Northwest. We have a lovely dinner, and I am investigated by three cats curious about my presence.

I sort of volunteer to join Cuong and Jackie and a few of their friends to celebrate New Year's Eve in a novel way. We drive and park along the bank of the Willamette River and walk across on one of Portland's many bridges towards downtown. It is a strange feeling to look at the cold, quiet river below in the dead of night. We approach the Salmon Street Springs, one of my favorite spots in the summer, and participate in the annual Midnight 5K Walk/10K Run, benefiting a local charity. We choose the "5K" option, thank God. As we walk, we see quite a few dogs, which, I can tell, are absolutely thrilled to be "out for a walk" at this time of night. Wagging tails and sniffing muzzles abound. At the finish line, there is bottled water for the participants, both two- and four-legged. We head home and enjoy a little champagne, sharing good wishes for the new year to come.

In the late morning, I get my first glimpse of the house in the daytime. As I look at the backyard and notice a tree, Cuong explains to me that he has had to trim back his walnut tree quite a bit, much to the dismay of the local squirrels. He has, however, replaced the missing branches with a squirrel feeder, which offers a rather amusing treat called "Squirrel Delight". I observe a rather gluttonous squirrel "delighting" himself. From his, shall we say, plump appearance, he appears to be a frequent visitor.

As afternoon approaches, I say good-bye, and drive to visit my oldest friends, Patrick and Sanae, in Beaverton. Oh, what a pleasure it is to see old friends. We catch up on things and go to bed late.

The next day is busy for both Patrick, who has to go to open his restaurant, and for Sanae, who is going to work; so I embark on a drive I have always wanted to take. I have seen some of the Columbia River due east, but never its mouth. Headed north, I drive through Portland, crossing the Washington border. I take a map this time, and the little dots on it promising a scenic route keep their word. With every mile as I turn west, the sprawling gray river gets wider,.Fishermen stand by the banks next to their parked pick-up trucks, obviously enjoying their passion despite the brisk weather. Driving by two small towns with the Indian names of Cathlamet and Skamokawa, it is apparent why the towns are situated on this river: the views are stunning. The scene makes me think of a book I read as a young boy about the Lewis and Clark expedition.

The road now wanders away from the river to a more coniferous landscape, slightly hilly and then gradually spreading out. I continue along Willapa Bay to the Long Island Peninsula, deserving its name, as the map visually informs me. The sun is low on the horizon but still bright on this late winter afternoon. The peninsula gives me the impression that it would be a busy seaside resort in the summer. I park on the beach near the sand dunes, seagulls swirling overhead. A few bright kites are also in the air, frolicking about delightfully. The clerk in one of many kite stores informs me that in the summer there is a huge kite festival here, attracting enthusiasts from all over the world. A postcard showing literally thousands of kites in the air proves the point. Further south in the port town of Ilwaco, several large fishing boats rest their wooden hulls on stilts in the dry winter air, waiting patiently to be painted so they will be ready once again for another year of fishing. Past Chinook, I come to the mouth of the Columbia River. Looking at the vastness of the river, I slowly make my way along the bank, then cross a seemingly endless tall bridge toward Astoria on the Oregon side. Time for a bite to eat and for a bit of a Northwest specialty: smoked salmon.

The sun is in my favor, so I continue south towards Highway 26, which promises to take me back to Portland. Heading west, the green forests of Oregon engulf me. It is close to dusk, and from a distance the birch trees look almost like cotton candy. Further south, the now black evergreens silently border the road which goes on for what seems like hours, its darkness interrupted occasionally by a few headlights. As the road turns due east, the highway signs start to announce impending arrival in the City of Roses. I manage not to get lost this time. I pick up Cuong and Jackie, and we head for da Vinci's for dinner. Thank you for feeding us, Patrick! After dropping off my friends, I head back to Beaverton to keep Jiro, the seaweed-eating cat, company, until Patrick and Sanae come home. I love how cats can put on that "haven't been fed for a week" look and think they can get away with it.

The next day sees a glorious 49er victory, which Patrick unfortunately has to watch from the kitchen at da Vinci's, after making some breakfast for us in Beaverton.

The days pass quickly, and Monday is here in no time. Patrick and I talk for a bit in the house, and then we take Sanae to lunch. No trip to Portland is complete for me without seeing the Japanese Gardens. It's my first time there in winter. I see the koi I'm so fond of moving sluggishly as they sleep at one edge of the pond, perhaps dreaming of sunny spring days. Back once more to Beaverton to say good-bye, then to the airport. Until we meet again.

Passport OK, bags checked in with the poor girl who has to struggle to lift the behemoths, and it's off to the gate. The plane is almost full of passengers coming from Tahiti who still have a long flight ahead of them to Paris, unlike us lucky stragglers climbing on board here in Oakland who only have to fly half the distance. Once again technology defies gravity as the huge 747 lumbers into the evening sky.

After a dinner with the choice of chicken or chicken (such interesting menu choices), I go to the back of the plane to investigate a duty-free item I spotted earlier in the on-board magazine. A smiling flight attendant greets me, and I ask her if the thermal bag I saw in the magazine works with ice like a cooler. *Non*, she replies, then opens the bag, grabs a water bottle and stuffs it inside the bag, swinging it over her shoulder and walking a bit, and in a singsong voice talks about going to the beach. *Très amusant,* and definitely an easy sale.

The night passes quickly, and below us Paris ORLY airport comes into view. I think it should be obligatory for airlines arriving in France to pump air smelling of *café au lait* and *croissants* into the cabin prior to landing. Once again I have the privilege of renting a Twingo, and the shuttle driver takes me to pick me up to La Bleue Deux, an exact twin to her sister of the year before. Despite the multitude of maps of Paris on the front seat, I find my accommodations by instinct again, and as luck would have it, that includes a parking space in front of the hotel. Not bad for a tourist. After several trips in the sardine-can elevator to bring the bags to the fifth floor, I finally heave a sigh of relief at having arrived. Opening the window to take in the view, I see on the street below my friend Patrick who had flown in earlier from Oregon.

Waving from above, I soon greet him with a big hug after descending in *le petit ascenseur* again. We look for and find Patrick's wife Sanae, and together head out for our first dinner at the "Tramway du Lyon". The waitress and owner must have detected the cameras of the tourists -- they produce English menus. I, however, insist on a French one to see if nine months of classes did any good. The steak that arrives is not horse or donkey. So far so good; at least the basics seem to have stuck. After a long and enjoyable meal, we all agree to meet in the early morning.

The *Métro* takes us several stops through a sleepy Sunday Paris to La Tour Eiffel. The lines at the ticket counters are still short at this early hour. Below the feet of the tower, whose immensity is in no way done justice to on postcards, several African street vendors are displaying mechanical birds in flight by tossing them into the air. The noise of the wings is especially enticing. Children's eyes will soon lead to voices badgering their parents to buy one.

After a short wait in line, we make our way to the first platform by means of an angled elevator, an engineering marvel and curiosity. The view from here is already spectacular. A soccer game in progress below turns into a game of toy players at this height. The white and ivory colored apartment houses so typical of Paris crowd the skyline, as a hot air balloon rises in the distance. Parks laid out in perfect symmetry delight the eye. The next elevator takes us all the way to the top platform, where inside a small booth Gustave Eiffel, recreated in wax, can be seen in simulated animated conversation. Graffiti on the unique brown colored steel beams surround his habitat. The painters no doubt are blessed with patience to work on a structure such as this. Foreign languages from all parts of the globe can be heard as tourists in sometimes amazingly bizarre attire circle the small platform.

As we arrive back at the foot of the tower again, long lines have now formed at the ticket booths. A French policewoman on a bicycle chases away one of the bird vendors, who retreats back to the perimeter of the sidewalk, where it seems he will be safe from prosecution. Apparently it's an endless game of cat and mouse.

Boarding a Paris attraction, L'OpenTour, one of the bright tree frog colored double decker buses that are open on top, we embark on a tour of the city. I believe there is no better way to get a first impression of the city, as you can get a great overview. What perhaps makes this tour special is that one can get off and back on at any stop along the way. A low-flying-sparrow perspective and an unobstructed camera view from the top level are an added bonus. After looking at numerous monuments, palaces and museums, the eyes start to blur and the stomach, true to French custom, takes over, suggesting lunch.

Having perused an entire guidebook the night before, Patrick suggests a restaurant near Notre Dame. "A favorite with Americans," it claims, and although a European citizen, I agree to sample it. After being ignored for a while and then denied a seat at a table in the shade, we are finally seated, then get to wait for water. I do manage to use the rest room, though this seemingly proves a great hindrance to the passing and oh-so-busy waiter. Disgusted, we depart. I think we should leave this gem of hospitality to the next American tour bus, with any luck containing a professional football team both hungry and mean.

After a short walk across one of the bridges of the Seine, we find a charming outdoor cafe with an excellent menu and waiters intent on proving their humor. Across the street a giant television screen has been set up in anticipation of tonight's European soccer

À CÔTÉ DE GARE DE LYON

championship game between France and Italy. The waiter advises us of an expected stadium crowd of 30,000 or more spectators.

After lunch we walk off the calories past the Centre Pompidou, a building resembling an oil refinery and painted in bright colors. It's the legacy of the former French president Pompidou, who had the vision to tear down this block and turn it into a center for the arts, thus infusing new life into the city. A drizzle has us ducking under cover where we can see the fountains across from the center, a collection of brightly painted humorous shapes spouting water from their various openings and in multiple streams. An elephant of many colors is the winner, in my opinion.

An early evening *Métro* ride from the Gare de Lyon takes us into the center of town. We miss the last boat of a river tour, but a pleasant stroll along the Seine more than makes up for it. On a fireboat the crew can be seen sitting in front of a TV screen in anticipation of the big game. Another barge carries two dogs standing in front of the cabin door, eagerly wagging their tails. Must be dinner time. As luck would have it, we find a sports bar in time for the game. Thank you for your patience, Sanae. After a dramatic game ending in a French overtime victory, the people in the bar and on the streets begin a joyous celebration. "*Les Bleus, Les Bleus*" (the French team nickname) fills the air. Cries of "*Ont et les champions*" echo everywhere. Our attempt to take the *Métro* home is futile, however. The tracks are shut down with the fans having taken over the lower domains of the city. Waving flags, they run and jump over the turnstiles at stations heading who knows where. Exuberance everywhere, but peaceful. Late, and via a detour on the RER, we reach our beds in our hotel. The room's double windows can't keep out the sound of car horns, which seems to last until well into the morning.

Rise and shine. Early the next day La Bleue Deux performs her first duty, attempting to evade the Monday morning French meter maids. After a few kilometers on roads, cobblestone alleys take us up the rest of the way to the famous Montmartre district. We park next to the magnificent Sacre Cœur. Grateful for this trip and also in honor of my French sister-in-law, I light a candle inside this beautiful church. Outside, a street accordion player coaxing romantic melodies from his instrument gets the attention of Patrick and his camera. We stroll in search of a second *café au lait*, and a downpour of flood proportions ensues. The waiters struggle to keep the water flowing off the tops of the tents in the middle of the square, under which they have set up additional tables. The street painters look forlorn. Glimpses of umbrellas and makeshift rain gear of all kinds can be seen ducking for cover in the *cafés*. After finishing our coffee, we too dash in short spurts from building to building, finding our way back to the car during lapses in the rain. Thanks to my expert navigator and despite this weather spectacle, we swim down the alleys, and find refuge in an underground garage near the department stores of the Boulevard Haussman.

After the purchase of some *parapluies* (or umbrellas, if you must know), we find a Portuguese restaurant. I order a creamy seaweed soup with sausage pieces. Very interesting, and I use that phrase not in the way my grandmother did when she was trying to be polite. However, an attempt to educate the cook via the waiter on how to prepare broccoli (it was yellow) seems to fail, due to the language barrier.

The Grand French Department Stores beckon a visit. Before they swallow us, we walk past some sale tables out in front, where a lovely girl entices her customers with, "*allez-allez, oh-la-la, oh-la-la.*" On one of the upper floors of the store I find a culinary section. A few of its inhabitants later wind up in my suitcase (which the scales at the airport later would tend to confirm). The French specialties of *calvados*, *pastis*, jams and spices are irresistible. We meet downstairs and as we pass Mademoiselle "*oh-la-la, oh-la la*" again, I parrot an "*allez-allez*" to her. I receive an amused smile in return. It must be hard for her to do that all day long.

We store our culinary valuables in the Twingo, and as luck would have it find another L'OpenTour bus stop nearby. Due to my questionable navigation skills, however, we board the wrong one, and are now stuck on the route to Montmartre on the last bus of the day. Besides us, there is only one passenger on board, plus of course the driver, who has a hard time negotiating afternoon rush hour traffic. Finally it dawns on me that this morning attempting to read a newspaper, I figured out that "*Les Bleus*" were to have a parade on the Avenue des Champs Elysées. That, along with the storm, is responsible for this horrendous traffic backup throughout the entire city. With only occasional sprinkles now, Patrick and I head to the top of the bus to look at the sea of cars. Near one of the train stations, we come to a complete stop, and the cars refuse to let the bus join the line of traffic. Fed up, I go downstairs and ask the bus driver to open the doors. I then stop traffic and he manages to make the turn. A high-five later, I am back on the top of the bus. Early evening settles on the city as the bus drops us off at the last stop, the driver happy to head home. We find La Bleue Deux and our hotel gathers us tired tourists for the night. I am amused once again by the long sausage-shaped pillow on the bed, an item popular in France.

Our plan for today is to visit the gardens of Monet at Giverny, a plant and art lover's dream, but also the breeding place of tourist buses, according to a sarcastic visitor quoted in my French textbook. However, the sky is pitch black today, and at eight o'clock in the morning, it resembles night, as an unbelievable downpour hits the cobblestone streets. We manage to reach the *Périphérique* but are stuck in gridlock traffic, and finally decide to get off at the next exit, realizing that the rain won't stop. I suggest an alternate plan of visiting La Villete, formerly a 136-acre livestock market serving the whole of Paris. It is now a science city and park. Patrick, my navigator, is frustrated that the same street changes its name every so often on the map, but nonetheless he gets us there with precise directions such as "turn at one o'clock," as we traverse various complex intersections. I twingo us into a vast underground garage, and the elevator takes us to the top.

The main building hosts a rather impressive array of both science and technology exhibits. For some reason unknown to me, Patrick and I are drawn to the automobile section. An old Citroën DS-19, monitors displaying humorous French car company commercials spanning automotive history, and even a real live Twingo delight the eye. It's amazing how Twingos are built: the modular design is such that the car is assembled in two pieces, a top and a bottom segment that are then pushed together almost like you would put together a toy model. (Yes, I am enamored with Twingos, in case you haven't guessed yet.) After strolling through the halls, we meet outside at La Géode, a 100-foot-high geodesic dome that looks like a gigantic shiny marble and houses a 180-degree (hemispherical) movie screen. The rows of seats rise almost vertically. The 70mm film features sharks and other marine life in the Pacific Ocean off the coast of South America. Scenes change from underwater panoramas to bird's-eye views. It is breathtaking -- you feel completely immersed in the environment and you can experience the motion of flying and swimming in your stomach. I have never experienced anything like it.

The skies start to clear as we head to the center of Paris, again to the culinary district recommended in our illustrious guidebook. After another venture down into an overpriced underground parking garage, we come up for lunch near La Madeleine. An omelet that after two returns is still not worthy of its name (once too runny, the second time overcooked) really ticks off Patrick, who is almost ready to enter the kitchen and slap the buffoon upside the head to demonstrate how to make a proper one. I can understand his frustration, as he is a chef. Afterwards, we venture into the tea and gourmet shops. Patrick finds numerous delicacies for use in his restaurant, and Sanae discovers a pastry shop that uses surveillance cameras to protect its heavenly creations. A vendor in a fruit store encourages me to sample a small sweet banana, after we have brief conversation comparing France and California. They really have the freshest and finest fruit in Paris (from what I have tasted thus far).

After storing our edible delights in La Bleue Deux, we again take the

Métro, this time to the massive and imposing Arc de Triomphe, which we'd seen from afar days before. The Fourth of July warrants a French homage to the Americans of the second World War. French soldiers with uniforms representing French history stand near the Tomb of the Unknown Soldier as a military band waits to march and play. A *gendarme* is kept busy keeping the crowds back behind the line of procession. After the ceremony, we climb the 282 steps leading to the top of the Arc. It's worth the long climb; the streets laid out below in a star shaped pattern are a magnificent sight. A kaleidoscope of cars travels up and down them and then scoots around the Arc in a dizzying frenzy. Patrick has to almost drag me away from the top, as I can't get enough of watching this.

Ready for dinner, the Twingo operator is put in charge of finding a restaurant Patrick and Sanae visited the year before. After a few detours, and finding a parking spot whose legality may be subject to debate, we walk the rest of the way to our destination. Most of the French cuisine of the last few days has been a delight (my editor has a note here that says I'm thinking of that omelet -- the one blatant exception), but the meal tonight at Le Relais Saint-Paul, a name I am proud to mention in this story, is exceptional. We dine on, among other treats, seafood *mousse soufflé* with caramelized onions, a salad with grapefruit juice, honey, and warm cheese, and *paté* with jellied *consommé*. Are you hungry yet?

After finishing our last Parisian *petit déjeuner* the next morning, we take a small trip to purchase some travel provisions at "our" corner store, then head to a French laundromat. One machine, we discover, is used for removing excess moisture from washed clothes, spinning them at a much higher speed than the normal spin-cycle of a regular washing machine. It seems a worthwhile budget and time consideration, proving again that travel broadens the horizons. Two trips to the Gare de Lyon deliver my friends and their suitcases to their train (it should be probably be noted that I take several wrong turns to reach the station the first time, but by repeating those same wrong turns faithfully on the second trip I again arrive at the station). Then comes the always hard good-bye.

After I gather my suitcases, the *Périphérique* takes me away from Paris streets to the *Autoroute,* destination Germany. Many kilometers later, the fields of summer come into view on both sides, golden patches of wheat meeting a darkening sky fighting the last afternoon sunlight. I thankfully ponder the joyous past few days as I head east to see my parents and brothers.

Distances look so small on a colorful map, but increase as the actual driving ensues. After an early morning departure from München, I make a stopover in a small village near Augsburg to visit my godfather. A planned half-hour visit turns into a few hours and an invitation to lunch -- sausages and pretzels with mustard, a Bavarian specialty. Saying good-bye in the early afternoon, I navigate toward the mountainous roads of the Weinstraße with their high slopes of picturesque vineyards silhouetted against an unusual August sky of gray drizzle.

Past Saarbrücken, *et voilà*: France once again, the Twingo knows its way home. Because it is late afternoon already, I reluctantly take the *Autoroute* rather than the much-preferred country roads. I keep thinking of what I saw near my friend Dirk's house in München, an elephant right smack in the middle of a farmer's field and yes, I did try to bring him some peanuts and got yelled at by his trainer. Part of a traveling circus, he seemed quite out of place there -- but what a sight to behold.

Alsace-Lorraine: the endless golden fields to the left and right and the smell of fresh hay make it an easy early-evening drive. Exiting the *Autoroute* after driving for several hours, and believing this to be the location of a motel recommended to me, I come to a town that seems more like an American tourist resort than an authentic French village. I didn't come here for this, so off we go. Taking a side road and stopping for some "*sans plomb*" in a depressing, almost-abandoned industrial town, I decide to head back to the *Autoroute* in the hope of finding the "real" France. I must admit that driving so many kilometers today has taken its toll on me. As the sun sets, the tops of the wheat stalks take on a last bright summer glow. I exit at the sign for Châlons en Champagne, and the outskirts of town appear. How strange, it seems so empty everywhere. I find a hotel and the clerk helps me with the heavy luggage as I make my trips to and fro from my Twingo.

The mystery of the empty town is revealed later as I walk into the town square in search of a late dinner. The entire population of the town seems to be there, listening to a summer musical rendition on a stage set up in the center. Dinner and a cold *pastis* hit the spot after the long drive. It's fun to see the French kids greet each other with kisses on both cheeks. The *pastis* makes for easy slumber.

The smell of *croissants* and coffee drifts through the hotel hallway. A young sleepy-eyed boy and a small dog are downstairs between the hallway and breakfast room. I am found acceptable with a sniff of the small nose and reciprocate with a pat on the head for *le petit chien*. The boy gets some melon candy.

On the road again. It's still chilly and gray, but the small roads through the Champagne are a pleasure to drive. In every little town champagne bottles hang from the buildings, advertising their bubbly contents. A side road along the hills of grapes takes me to a *château* that is out of reach, guarded by a tall iron fence. The view through the bars is splendid, though -- what a feat of architecture. One can only marvel that such a grand structure took decades or centuries to build.

Passing a few dozen more champagne bottle signs, I finally stop at one. A large mural depicting a vintner tending his vineyards covers the front of the building. On one side I spot a fox fondly looking at the grapes. Inside the building, the air is cold. An adorable puppy about the size of my hand and curled up in a blanket attracts my attention. After I pet it, it follows me everywhere. The owner comes through the back door and I ask him in Level 4 French if I may purchase a small bottle of champagne from him, letting him know that I am from California. A smile comes to his face: "Ah, *Californie*, Napa Valley," he repeats, as he invites me back to take a look at his cellar. He and his wife are in the process of filling the champagne bottles, putting in the corks, and then covering them with golden foil. I am grateful for this "insider" peek at the process. Outside I take Monsieur Boilleau's picture, with his puppy in pursuit. He informs me that it is now time for it to go "*peepee*," which it promptly attends to. I wave goodbye, happy that I stopped.

Negotiating the *Péripherique* around the outskirts of Paris, I drive a short stretch of *Autoroute* towards my final destination for the night: Ducey on the Salune river near the Normandie coast. Fed up with constantly paying tolls, I decide to take the secondary roads marked in red in *Bibendum,* the Michelin man's atlas of France. The afternoon sun peeks through the clouds. Gigantic harvesters on the roads often cause long backups for the traveling vacationers; one has to acknowledge the priority of their work. Since the summer has been so rainy, the farmers have to take advantage of every dry opportunity to bring in the harvest of wheat, providing our daily bread.

After a very long drive through lower Normandie, I finally spot a road sign announcing imminent arrival in Ducey. Entering the small town, the weary traveler is greeted by tiny French flags strung from building to building across the streets in anticipation of a summer festival this weekend. I check into the bed & breakfast, then opt for a stroll before dinner. Evening has settled on the town. A cat running on the ledge underneath the second floor of a building grabs my attention. As it approaches a window, the shutters open and it dashes inside, the shutters closing quickly behind it. Very amusing, and an oft-practiced routine by cat and owner, it appears. Back at my bed & breakfast for dinner, I see a postcard depicting a Normandie cow on the counter. It's a very picturesque cow. The text, my dictionary later helps me understand, says the four-footed creature is allowed to step on the grass without fear of reprimand. An exquisite meal in the dining room brings to a close the long day. Although not from the Salune, the smoked salmon is heavenly. Back in my room, having gained experience that early rising is wholesome and has its benefits, I set the clock appropriately for the next day.

What a difference. Gazing out the window I'm greeted by a heavy fog thick as pea soup which lies over the river and town. By the time I finish a delicious breakfast, the fog has lifted a bit. My Twingo is eager to get on the road again, having been confined to her parking enclosure for the night. The grass along the windy country roads glistens with dew. I am on my way to famous Le Mont-Saint-Michel. The first rays of sun peek out behind the clouds, although it is still hazy. I stop by the roadside to take a few pictures of a stand that sells *calvados*, the famous apple brandy of Normandie. I arrive early at my destination, and a few sleepy parking attendants direct me to a space below the monastery, a short walk away. I join a few other early morning tourists and wade through the ebb tide taking pictures of the sea and sand surrounding this great landmark, as I'm sure millions have done before me. A dog chases some seagulls who voice their displeasure in no uncertain terms.

I reach the obligatory admission booth. Inside the monestary, a narrow medieval passage winds upwards. To the left and right are tourist trinket and souvenir shops squeezed into every nook and cranny. The smell of the sea and its denizens pervades the air. Delivery people trudge on the cobblestones bringing in supplies. A chef is preparing for the day, a sign in front of him advertising fresh mussels and seafood omelets. After I've walked a few hundred feet, a small passage off to the right affords a spectacular view through a window. The sea, in colors ranging from fog to sandpiper, is encroaching upon the sands surrounding this magnificent island. Flocks of seagulls sporadically dive down in search of a marine breakfast. Due east, the first tour buses can be seen invading. I'm glad I got up early. After reaching the top, I too take a tour of the monastery: often dark cavernous rooms, at other times bright, sometimes lit by the sun filtering through the stained glass windows. People are quiet and respectful. A narrow path leads past a garden and a cemetery, and ends at one of the small passages leading downward again, where the entrance area is now jam-packed. A policeman on a forklift toots the horn and is reluctantly granted passage by the advancing horde of sightseers. Outside in the parking lot, my Twingo is now completely surrounded by cars.

Leaving, I stray off on a side road past a few stone houses and come to a dead end near the sea. Because of the low tide, most of the muddy ground is visible. In the distance, I see a few brightly-dressed people holding something in their hands. My telephoto lens reveals fishermen holding nets attached to two poles on either side that they dip into the sea and then lift up again. A peculiar way to fish.

After a stop to buy some bread and wine, I drive north along the coast past stone houses typical of Normandie -- sometimes sitting iso-lated, sometimes congregating in small villages. Live versions of the picturesque brown and white postcard cow are standing about. I moo at a few them with what I deem to be a French accent and am greet-ed with a look of "*touriste stupide*". It is strange to see lush green pastures right next to the sea. Every small village I pass has at least one sign touting *calvados*. Le Mont-Saint-Michel can still be seen in the far distance, attesting to its size.

The coastal road brings me to the summer seaside resort of Jullouville. I park on a street covered with drifting white sand and wander down to the beach. Several tractors are towing small sailboats on trailers in and out of the water. A very practical solution on the sand, and what looks like to be a great summer job. The drivers of the tractors eye me with curiosity wondering what on earth I am taking pictures of; it seems that for them it is nothing special.

I arrive in Granville, which lies on a peninsula, and as I round the corner near the center of town, two gigantic deep sea buoys sitting inside a large shipyard beckon for a stop. I estimate them to be at least an impressive two stories tall. Up the road, a thick storm wall surrounds the fishing fleet in the harbor, leaving only a small opening for the boats to make their journey out into the Atlantic. Stuck in the mud of the harbor because of the low tide, the stragglers lie tilted on their sides. They remind me of helpless fish flopping about after being caught. Circling the upper end of town, I come to a fortress that bears homage to the Second World War. A few turrets and plaques serve as a grim reminder.

Parking on the harbor road with a view of now completely stranded fishing boats, I decide on a *"fruits de mer"* lunch, crusty and slippery inhabitants of the sea in a delicious combination. A postcard educates me as to their French names. I ask the waitress about the harbor walls, and she tells me that the storms in the fall and spring can be intense and frightening when the sea unleashes all its fury. Afternoon sun guides me back to Ducey for a nap after this eventful day, followed later by an early bedtime.

My intention is to visit Honfleur this morning, having seen it in a movie many years ago. Bicyclists are out on the country roads, perhaps inspired by the Tour de France. I stop in the tiny village of Tourgeville to photograph several houses with grass growing on thatched roofs and windows decorated by blue shutters. "Quaint" seems an appropriate description. A bell rings for Sunday service, and I turn around to see a little church inviting me in through worn but open wooden doors. The stained glass windows cast a blue glow. I can't understand much, but melodious French hymns float through the air. Refreshed, I continue my journey.

Past Deauville, heavy noon traffic takes me to Trouville, a part fishing, part coastal resort town. The sky won't clear today; it's temperate, although not quite swimming weather. Unable to find a parking spot, and I need to mention that God usually provides those to me (I think I forgot to ask), I drive up a long hill, *et voilà*. Strolling downhill I spot an oval shaped turnout which displays a mosaic representation of Trouville. Below the walls that hold back the hill are grand mansions, probably from the 19th century, sitting right next to the sea, separated from it only by a long beach boardwalk. Climbing down-ward, I come to the boardwalk, which stretches along the entire beach. What a joy to wander along it. The atmosphere is subdued because of the weather, but people and a few dogs are out and about nonetheless. The color of the sand is a warm white. Past a poster of some seagulls lounging in beach chairs and advising against littering, a right-angled turnoff from the boardwalk takes me into the center of town. Perhaps inspired by the poster, I decide on lunch at "Les Mouettes," with the seagulls circling above giving applause for the good choice. A delicious salmon is followed by an apple tart and the waiter brings me a *calvados* to top it off, insisting that this is obligatory. Thus I am well prepared for the climb back uphill, but first I take the boardwalk again. Strolling along I meet a little girl who is sitting on the sand and coloring seashells with magic markers. She

TROUVILLE — NORMANDIE
FRANCE

has been quite busy, as a good dozen of them surround her. She motions for me to take one, smiles at me and tells me, *"C'est gratuit."* Oh, what a sweetie. Choosing a shell, I encourage her to feed her piggy bank by giving her a few francs. Stopping halfway up the hill and turning to look at the sea, I talk a bit with a woman about the weather this summer. She tells me it's usually sunny, and that Trouville is her very favorite resort, which she loves to visit every year in order to escape the humidity of Paris.

Honfleur is a bit disappointing. Unlike the romantic portrayal I saw in the movie *Tendre Poulet*, it is a tourist town with heavy summer traffic. The one consolation prize is seeing the fishing boats painted in bright colors in the inner harbor.

You probably know the feeling of joy upon seeing something new when traveling, but this can sometimes lead to absentmindedness. I should have filled my tank in Honfleur but figure there will be something along the way, forgetting that it's Sunday and customary for many gas stations in France to remain closed. Running on empty after stopping by several closed ones, I find a 24-hour automatic station. However, my credit card doesn't seem to be compatible with the French pumps. I ask two girls in the car next to me who are about to leave if they can help me. We agree on a credit card-for-currency exchange. I am very thankful and they are delighted by some raspberry candies I still have from California.

Adieu, Normandie. A last breakfast at the little bed & breakfast and it's off to Paris for the return flight. Brown and white cow faces silently munching lush grass in preparation to make milk and butter bid me farewell. No communication is attempted this time by *monsieur "touriste stupide"*.

A few hours later I find a car wash, and although it's not an Elephant Bleu as hoped for, I clean my Twingo until she is spotless.

Harvesters dot the fields again, as the sun has decided to come out. The winding Seine River takes me to Giverny, the place I missed when traveling with Patrick and Sanae. A sign pointing to Monet's gardens prompts a walk along a high stone wall, where I encounter a few other tourists from whom I receive sheepish looks. Wondering why, I come to the entrance, where a sign explains that Mr. Monet, or at least the caretakers of his garden, rest on Mondays. Not to be discouraged, I round the entire perimeter of the garden along the wall, and see an open truck trailer parked along the side. A quick climb up, and at least I am afforded a partial look over the fence into the gardens, a high-level inspiration, if you'll pardon the pun, for perhaps a future visit.

Afternoon again already. I decide on the *Autoroute* for the last stretch back into Paris in the direction of La Défense. It's *péage* time again, which, however, is justified by an enormously long tunnel that seems to go on forever but then lets out at the maze of roads surrounding La Défense, the futuristic new section of the city. Paris is strangely quiet, giving credence to the notion that most of its inhabitants flee to the sea in the month of August (remember, I found one of them in Trouville). This time, the city doesn't evoke the same joy I felt when I explored it with my best friends for a few days in July. It feels a little empty.

I arrive at the hotel, and I sympathize with the occupation of mover after managing my behemoth of a suitcase up several flights of stairs. It's also laundry time again. I find a laundromat a few blocks away and chat with a few American teenage girls as the machines practice their hypnotic round-and-round. One of the girls is somewhat unacquainted with the process as she opens the door of a washing machine, takes out her clothes and dumps them into another washing machine rather than a dryer across the room. This brings out some chuckles and comments from us all.

French fries, a hamburger and a milkshake are the French *pièce de résistance* for dinner at the fine French restaurant Hippopotamus. It brings back memories of Hippo Hamburgers a long time ago in San Francisco. Sometimes simple food can be the best. The night air is warm and humid as I head back to the hotel. Gazing out at the sky through the windows of the room, there is still no breeze to be felt, but the city of lights does its nickname justice.

That Is a Crack, This Is a Repair
Spring 2001

A morning walk in the California spring: poppies unfolding in the sun, a fence covered with sweet-smelling jasmine. A squirrel, turbo-charged in my opinion, races up a telephone pole. A humming-bird whizzes by as I open the door to the coffee store. A long line -- could this be the post office? Nope, it smells too good for that.

A neighbor is kind enough to give me a ride to the Castro Valley BART station, and from there it is an easy ride to the San Francisco Airport. After a flight free of turbulence, even during mealtimes, I arrive in Philadelphia.

Blue turnpike signs, as opposed to green freeway signs, direct me to the outskirts of Philadelphia. I arrive in the town of Ardmore where, after getting lost several times in the pitch dark, I find my son Christian's college dorm, thanks to his directions and to my mobile phone (that marvel of modern technology). After a short chat and a glimpse into his dwellings, I make my way to the bed & breakfast that will put me up for the weekend. As I travel down the "Main Line," as the road is called (a reference to railroad days), the directions printed out from the Internet prove worth their salt. A charming couple, along with their cat Toby, greet me in their home. I don't recall the species of cat, but if you held him upside down, he would just hang there, giving an opossum a run for its money.

After a delicious breakfast that includes home baked scones and mushrooms, which I am told grow in abundance here in Pennsylvania, I step outside to make my way back to the dorm to wake up my son. The landscape is a stark contrast to California: the trees are all bare, and a cold, clammy mist hangs overhead. Four seasons are the norm here. The houses are far apart and have large yards with old trees. As I head up the "Main Line," a Dunkin Donuts store catches my eye. More than fond of them, I must make a pit stop. I arrive again in Ardmore/Haverford and Christian gets to hold up the bag of donuts in a "photo opportunity".

Our plan for today is to visit Philadelphia. My rental car with its unique new Pennsylvania world wide web address on the license plate takes us down the "Main Line" again towards downtown. After a few miles, the outskirts come into view. I am dumbfounded: burned out buildings, trash everywhere; it's hard to believe this is really in the U.S. I have never seen anything like it in California. I think that from an architectural perspective a lot of the buildings are quite nice; with a little TLC they could be homes again. A parking space presents itself when we arrive downtown, and after getting some change from a candy vendor, we are now "legal". Despite this being his second year here, Christian has not seen the historical landmarks that make this city so famous. I guess it takes a tourist to accomplish this (it took me 27 years to see Alcatraz). Our first stop is the Liberty Bell. A queue winds into the street despite the brisk air (native Californians would have dropped like flies already), all of us eagerly awaiting a glimpse of U.S. history. Once we're inside, a park ranger of prominent stature with the voice of a marine sergeant to back it up, has us gather round. He corrects a much-maligned myth about the "crack" in the bell: it is not what it seems, but a "repair" to alleviate the pressure from the real crack a few inches from the top of the bell. To the bemusement of the tourists, he repeats this point several times with great emphasis. No, no miniature versions were bought in the gift shop, I can promise. Around the corner, Independence Hall is the second stop. After another short queue, our ranger does an excellent job of presenting history as we admire the beautifully maintained interior of the building. My question about the significance of the different colors of the rooms, however, remains unanswered; perhaps it was a whim of the architect at the time.

Outside again, the sleeping trees and cool wind let it be known that spring is yet to come, a few forsythias around the square hinting that it's not far off. Off to the side is Flag Street. A "native" corrects my misconception of this being a street of embassies, and tells me that the flags are a whim of the local residents. For lunch, we head to South Street, the culinary pathway to "cheese steaks," your arteries' best friend.

After walking back and retrieving the car, we pick up some take-out chicken for dinner. As the evening progresses, back at the dorm, it becomes clear that this particular apartment has an open door policy, as friends come and go. After a few conversations I decide to head back to my b&b; it's getting late.

The next morning, after attending a service in Haverford, I make my way to wake up Christian. Thanks to a neighbor, I gain entry, and after several attempts manage to wake the sleepyhead.

Navigating the Pennsylvania turnpikes, we arrive in Flourtown, at the home of friends of my father's from over 35 years ago. After a delicious breakfast with the O'Hares, they take us on a drive to visit the house I lived in as a ten-year-old in Fort Washington. For some reason I never forgot the address, perhaps because it rhymed: 7032, Lafayette Avenue. It's a strange feeling to see something from so long ago. Our next stop is a park and trail along the Wissahickon Creek, more like a small river at this time of year -- gurgling currents rushing past large white boulders. A forgotten purple hat sits on a fence post nearby. After a nice late lunch near Chestnut Hill, we say goodbye and head off towards Longwood Gardens, whose name was oft-heard from my mother, the avid gardener.

The outside is bleak and gray, a still dormant landscape. Inside the greenhouses, fragrances are intense. We step into a different climate, yellow fragrant mimosas taking up an entire greenhouse. Another hall has a vibrant collection of orchids in every color imaginable. The Mediterranean Gray Garden has only plants in every shade of gray. Bonsai adorn another greenhouse. The lushness and smells are intoxicating. Unfortunately, having arrived late, we have to leave after only a short visit. Along the path, a sign on a tree tells its story of having been moved to this location by helicopter, quite a trip for a botanical specimen.

Arriving back in Haverford, I get the dusk tour of the campus, a duck pond glistening in the distance. After a long Goodbye, I backtrack to the home of the O'Hares, who are kind enough to put me up for the night. We go shopping, then cook dinner together; my share is my mother's herb butter recipe, which always seems to find favor whenever made. A basketball game on TV, and it's off to bed.

The morning presents a surprise: snow! everywhere! OK, OK, so we have it in Tahoe too, but for a Bay Area resident it still is always a novelty and delight. Bob and I take a drive back to the Wissahickon Creek, where he jogs six miles every other day. I opt for the walking approach, being of a somewhat more sluggish nature. The branches of the trees are all covered with wisps of snow, and small flurries rush past here and there. A red barn spans the creek and marks the turnaround point. As I get back into the car, I spy the purple hat still sitting on its fence post, longing for its owner to retrieve it. Good-bye, thank you for the hospitality!

Petit Tour de France
Summer 2001

A warm sunny day in San Francisco, one of the few days that you can actually sit outside here and bask in the summer sun. I just finished watering the Sunday School planter boxes with their sunflowers and morning glories outside the kitchen of St. Matthew's. I have been sleeping in the church for a few months now, after vacating my room in a prior residence and putting my stuff into storage, and I'm very happy to take a break to go visit my family in Germany. Life has been more than stressful. I get a ride to the Oakland airport, where I meet my sons. They are as excited as I am about our trip.

The unusual nighttime departure makes for a late afternoon arrival. A rather amusing sight greets us on the luggage conveyer belt in ORLY. First, a dog in a container arrives through the entry door, and then, after a short pause, a cat comes through. Both are warmly greeted by their owners. The space between the arrival time of the dog and the cat seem to have been timed just right, so as to minimize friction between the two. I would venture to guess they didn't have a choice of "chicken or beef," though, and are most likely not too fond of flying.

It's funny to see some of the people that came from Tahiti, the origin point of the flight before the stopover in Oakland, walking barefoot inside the Paris airport terminal. For the first time in years we are stopped by customs, where they suspiciously look at Patrick's bass and my guitar. It turns out the inspector is a music fan, and after some chit-chat about guitars, he smiles and waves us through.

For space reasons, I have rented a Renault Kangoo this time, which, in addition to us three big galoots, will transport my brother and god-daughter later on during the trip. Patrick suggests naming our rental Kangoo "Tubby," a name which I frequently confuse with "Dumpy," but nonetheless a very apt name. I sure do miss having a Twingo, though. To make up for it, I greet all the other Twingos on the road, with "Twingo!", much to the delight of my offspring.

After finding our hotel and depositing the luggage, we head out for dinner. Oh, what a blessing to sit on a quiet side street in Paris at dusk, pondering the evening menu. If memory serves me well (which it often doesn't), we had *croque madame* and an exquisite filet of sole.

I manage to convince Patrick and Christian to get up early to avoid the crowds, and the location of our hotel allows us to walk to the Tour Eiffel after a breakfast of coffee and *croissant*s. There is only a small queue at the elevator entrances. Hazy light filters through the trees surrounding the large open space at the approach to the Tour. I don't see the mechanical bird vendors from last year, but the trinket and postcard vendors seem to have doubled in number. I'm looking forward to showing my sons the tower, which I enjoyed so much when I visited with Patrick and Sanae. The shutters of the ticket booths open, and after purchasing our tickets, we take the elevator to the top of the tower with stops on the way. At the top observation point, Patrick climbs and clings onto the fence with all fours, a great photo opportunity (which would most likely be frowned upon by the guardians of the tower if they were witness to it). After riding the elevator to the next platform below, we decide to walk down the rest of the steps, greeted by the huffing and puffing of the climbers who are taking the hard way up. I start counting steps, but lose count after a while. The perspective is quite fun, and it's less crowded than the elevator. At the last platform, there is a photo exhibit of the tower and its history, including highlights of the various exhibitions of light that have illuminated the tower, the *pièce de resistance* being the year 2000 celebration. I find a Tour Eiffel replica made out of sugar with banana flavoring in the gift shop for Camille, my navigator-to-be later on this summer. Afterwards, L'OpenTour, one of the double-decker buses that are open on top, takes us for a grand tour of the city. Dinner near our hotel marks the day's end.

Our guidebook promises fresh air and botanical splendor at the Jardin du Luxembourg, and after breakfast we take Tubby and navigate towards it through the maze of Paris streets. As luck would have it, we find parking right next to the gardens on a back street. The morning sun filters through the buildings as we walk past some firemen washing down the cobblestone streets. As we walk through the entrance gate, two symmetrical rows of chestnut trees greet us on both sides. The sun fills their green leaves with translucency. Patrick finds a statue of a lion, reflecting our family name. The gardeners are quietly starting their day. Orange and palm trees in large wooden containers are interspersed along the wide paths, enjoying their summer home outside. Taken for granted in California, these fine specimens were only the privilege of royalty not so very long ago. Walking under the chestnut trees, we hear fluttering and an occasional brawl, if such a term may be applied to birds. Upon closer view, they look somewhat like pigeons, but larger and pretty. Either Patrick or Christian, I don't recall who, decides to call them "royal pigeons". They are amusing, and appear rather territorial about their trees. As if from a postcard, a park bench draws me to bask in the sun. Its morning warmth is just glorious. My sons have a hard time getting me off the bench, and I play a little game with them, finding other benches to sit on once I get off one. I guess the fatigue of the last few months has just caught up with me.

Is it lunch time again already? We decide to retrieve some food we left in Tubby, and walk along the iron fence surrounding the Jardin. Funny, all the parking spots are now empty. Tubby is gone! We can't believe it. I bought a parking sticker from the machine and made sure it was a legal spot, so it shouldn't have been towed. Was Tubby kidnapped? I ask a *gendarme* down the street where the closest police station is, and he directs me about half a mile away to the other side of the gardens. Reaching the *gendarmerie*, I try to explain to the police about our Tubby, giving them the name of the street he was parked on. After a few telephone calls, the *gendarme* smiles and I learn that Tubby has been towed and deposited on another street just a few blocks away. I ponder this, and then it dawns on me; the firemen must be having some kind of celebration today and have cleared the streets for it. The *gendarme* grins broadly when I ask, *"Fête de pompiers?"* After getting directions on how to find Tubby, we head out the station doors. Sure enough, there he is, safe and sound. I guess putting up some signs to alert the ignorant tourist is harder than just towing. Go figure.

Jet lag makes a nap tempting, as we draw near our hotel. After buying a telephone card for Patrick and petting a German shepherd outside the *café*, we head to our respective rooms.

Christian doesn't wake up again until the next morning, and Patrick and I have dinner at a charming little restaurant in an alley that serves specialties from Provence. A dessert made of honey and lavender is the crowning touch.

Rise and shine, it's our last day in Paris. Remembering my prior visit, I want to show my sons the magnificent Arc de Triomphe. I decide the *Métro* is our best bet this time of day, as check-out time isn't until noon and we don't want to leave our stuff in the car. After figuring out the route on the large *Métro* map on the wall of the underground station, and then traversing a few passages, we see daylight again near the Arc de Triomphe. In somewhat better shape than last year, I manage to climb the steps to the top behind the speedy youths in front. Like last time, it is worth the long climb up; the view is *magnifique*. The area around the Arc is a beehive of morning busyness. Trucks, cars, motorcycles, buses, bicycles, delivery vans, and police cars circle the Arc. The stop-and-go, interweaving, intertwining flurry of activity is mesmerizing. A few crazy pedestrians actually run through this movement of vehicles. The vantage point from the top allows for excellent photographic capture of Twingos as well. On one street corner, several *gendarmes* stop vehicles, seemingly at random; perhaps the next morning's paper will shed light on their efforts.

We return to the hotel, and Christian and Patrick decide to pack, while I get a haircut across the street. My hairstylist, after managing to extract from me that I'm from California, peppers me with questions about the possibility of her moving and practicing her vocation there. I think she is half-serious, but more likely it's just daydreams. Sporting a clean summer head, I go to settle the bill at the hotel, and we load up Tubby. Our intended destination for today is Orléans (the original, not the "new" one).

After getting lost on the *Périphérique* a few times, we manage to find the road south. A stop at a *supermarché* fills our ice chest with plenty of picnic foods for the next few days. The matter of securing ice, however, proves rather elusive here in France. After I make several attempts to communicate the request for ice, one of the cashiers draws me a map of where to get some. *Merci!* Backtracking several kilometers, we find a giant store and park in the underground garage. Patrick and I head upstairs and proceed to chat with a fellow about ice. He is confused at first, but then calls a friend, who takes us to the back of the store. We are in the fish section, surrounded by our friends from the sea languishing on ice. The fishmonger gives us a bag and lets us scoop up ice from the huge piles the fish are lying on. After thanking him, we return upstairs and fill our ice chest. Let's hope our fruits and cheeses don't frolic in the fish-ice. Finally, after our last pit stop on the side of the road where Christian buys us some *pommes frites* with mayonnaise, we get the show on the road. The *Autoroute* leads south. We play a cat-and-mouse game with a Clio that sports bicycles on top. On the downhill stretches, Tubby proves to be the winner, perhaps due to -- how shall I put it -- a slight advantage in gross vehicle weight?

In the late afternoon, we reach the vicinity of the Loire. Then, taking the secondary roads for a while, I see what looks like a nice hotel in the rear view mirror. After a hand-brake turn worthy of *The Rockford Files* (oh, the joys of driving with a stick-shift and a hand-brake), we pull into the parking area in Châteauneuf-sur-Loire. The manager, informing us he has spent time in Florida, shows us our rooms, pointing out the amenities in English. He also helps us with our bags, as it is starting to drizzle. My room proves to have another of those unique French rest rooms. To say it could accommodate a pygmy would be kind. (I do hope that didn't go over your head, dear reader.)

After unpacking and a shower, we walk in search of dinner along the main road past a school with children's handprints on the front door. We settle on a pizza place. The proprietress greets us in French, but talks to us in English after listening to us chat. She is from England originally, but has lived here for a long time and is another California dreamer, as it turns out. After a delicious dinner of pizza and salad, we walk briskly to our hotel, slipping under the overhangs of the roofs where possible, as the slight drizzle has turned to rain.

The road outside our rooms, quiet last night, now bustles with morning activity. After breakfast and a short walk to the fruit and vegetable store next door to pick up some picnic items, we wake up Tubby. Our plan for today is to visit the famous *château* of Chambord (also the name of a raspberry liqueur). We cross a cattle grate of the *domaine* that encompasses Chambord, and Patrick gets to pose next to a sign which warns about wild boar, much to his delight. I'm sure Obelix, a character from the *Asterix* comics who is a wild boar gourmet, would have had no objections. It's drizzling again when we park, after maneuvering past the hordes of giant buses which have already gathered in the parking lot dispensing their tourists.

The *château* is magnificent. It's a maze of rooms, chambers, nooks, and apartments, interspersed with winding staircases and huge halls, all with white stone floors. The royal rooms are lavishly appointed. Enormous fireplaces in some and beautiful tapestries in others delight the eye. I tend to think it must have been a maid's nightmare to keep the place up. Tapestries and paintings depicting hunting scenes can be found in various rooms; it seems that was the main activity here during the past centuries. Rooms on the upper levels of the *château* offer panoramic views of the grounds. Chambord is proud of its title as the largest enclosed forest park in Europe. It was begun in 1519 and is a masterpiece of the French Renaissance. Once on the grounds outside, we pass by the chapel, and the obligatory gift shops loom large and demanding. I pick up a few postcards with recipes on them, but pass on the glass globe with Santa next to the Eiffel tower, as well as some pink toilet paper (presumably for the more non-discriminating *touriste*).

Still filled with ice and delectables, our *isotherme* beckons for a picnic. We make our way back to a spot we found near a small river with a brand new picnic table with a roof over it, and still smelling of fresh wood. There is nothing like a picnic in France: cheese, *paté*, ripe fruits and vegetables, a can of sardines, smoked trout, creamy butter, bread still fresh from the oven, and of course a glass of wine.

That evening we return to our now "favorite" pizza place, although if I recall correctly it is spaghetti we have this time. Yet another drizzle afterwards sends us scurrying back once again to our hotel.

The next morning, Tubby is packed, loaded and ready for some mileage. We cross the beautiful Loire over a long bridge, and stop in a picturesque town that has a small castle, complete with a moat. Inside the moat walls, there are small crevices, and pigeons are constantly flying in and out of them in various flight patterns. Riffraff no doubt, if you ask me, and untidy compared to their "royal" counterparts we encountered at the Jardin du Luxembourg.

The guidebook had mentioned Briare-le-Canal as the longest bridge canal in Europe, a phenomenon worth exploring and not far away. The bridge crosses the Loire and links two canals. Stonework and wrought-iron flourishes were designed by none other than Mr. Eiffel himself. After we climb up a small hill, the canal indeed appears, complete with a boat, making a postcard-worthy passage. It sure is a funny sight to see water flowing on a bridge.

Driving parallel to the Loire, we come to the Sancerre region, which from what I have read produces exquisite wines and the *Crottin de Chavignol,* their famous goat cheese. As luck would have it, we come upon a small farm that is advertised by a poster of a goat in a dress drinking wine. Both my sons comment on this bizarre spectacle. I wonder if the owner perhaps drank a bit too much of his own wine before selecting his advertisement. The proprietress is just about to close up, and we luck out in getting an herb goat cheese, some bread and a wonderful Sancerre white wine. An assortment of barn animals surrounds us during lunch. We thank these four-legged producers of the cheese, and depart.

Following the scenic route, Tubby meanders toward Limoges, which will be our stop for the night. Late in the afternoon, we are on a stretch of *Autoroute* when a downpour of biblical proportions hits us. I estimate that the cars which haven't stopped are crawling at 10 to 15 miles an hour on this normally speedy route. All things must pass, and later there is but a drizzle as we find a motel on the outskirts of Limoges. Parking Tubby next to an antique Citroën that could easily participate in a Commissaire Maigret movie, we check in and unpack. I faintly recall an unusual dinner of waffles.

Breakfast the next morning turns out to be a buffet, and after a tidbit of four *croissants* on my part, it's time to pack up and take a look at Limoges. After we purchase an umbrella and do the laundry, the skies clear a bit, and we walk down the street to one of the municipal buildings and view an exhibit of porcelain, the specialty of Limoges. In one section of the exhibit, a set of plates stick out of a layer of soil piled on the museum floor, an innovative way to display vegetables painted on porcelain. By venturing out to some side streets, I am able to purchase a few pieces that are more moderate in price than the ones in the exhibit, while my offspring find an internet *café* and are kept busy for a while. On the way back, we pass a store window with a collection of Matchbox and other toy cars with advertisements from past eras on them.

After we stock up on a few picnic items again, my navigator steers me in the direction of Périgeux, where my French teachers, Dominique and

Vanessa (who used to teach in San Francisco), live. After several phone calls, we meet up in busy Périgeux. They take us to the ruins of an old *colosseum*, and I take a photo on the "Rue du Gladiatores". Luckily the lions seem to be occupied elsewhere these days. Afterwards, we play a round of minigolf on a unique course that showcases castles and ruins from the region in miniature version. Dinner is in a seafood restaurant in the festively decorated old town. Paper flowers in beautiful colors are strung across the streets, reaching from window to window. It's the kind of fun summer spectacle put on by so many of the small towns in France. After consuming enormous platters of delicacies from the sea, we drive back to our hotel and say goodbye.

Today's plan is to reach the close proximity of La Merci Dieu where we will meet my brother, his wife Anne, my goddaughter Natascha, Madame du Hamel, and everyone else, not forgetting Jellie the plum-eating dog. It's been five years since we were last there.

After many hours of driving, I make a suggestion that is first opposed by my offspring because it seems to be "out of the way" on the map: to go through the region of Cognac, whose name has enticed me. We drive past endless fields of sunflowers smiling at us. When you take the small country roads in France you invariably encounter what is known in England as a "roundabout," which is a circle, rather than an intersection, where the roads meet. Not only does this solve traffic flow problems (as long as you know who has the right of way), but every circle is planted with colorful flower arrangements. My brother told me that the mayors of small towns make a "competition" out of this.

Driving through a suburb of Cognac, we make a brief pit stop at McDonald's, and no, not to dine but to get some ice for our *isotherme*. Perhaps I should mention that I am made aware for the first time by my sons of a dessert known as a McFlurry, an ice cream-like substance covered with M&Ms. That's too much to resist, and I send Patrick into the Golden Arches for said dessert as well as for some ice. In the meantime, I open up our ice chest and discover the hideous aroma of a cheese gone bad. I discreetly dispose of the offender on the steps of the front door of a building next to the car. Picturing the resident of the building retrieving his morning paper the next day, first sniffing the air and then gasping at the sad remains of the cheese, brings on a general tone of much bemusement for us. I sincerely doubt that another suggestion -- that an animal might come by and eat it -- would come about; no creature is that dumb. Stocked with fresh ice and McFlurries, we make our getaway.

Near the center of Cognac, we stop and enter a small distillery. Thick mortar walls make the cave-like room comfortably cool. The proprietress lets us sample a few of their aged and magnificent cognacs. I'm quite surprised when she lets Christian sample 50-year-old cognac, but it encourages a purchase. I think what strikes me most here is the quiet generosity about this great little place. Although it is already late afternoon, Christian insists on another stop at one of the "big" producers. Not only does Rémy Martin charge admission for the tour, but it is a non-stop self promotion and slick advertisement for the so-called "in" crowd. The whole place is fenced in and "security" guys with shades try to look cool in "guarding" everything. It is utterly pretentious, and the exact opposite of the quiet "cognac-for-a-special-occasion" place we visited before. I am really relieved to get out of there. This time I am outvoted when I suggest that we continue on to the ocean (which looks so nice and close on the map), and we agree to drive on the *autoroute* and stop in the town of Châtellerault. Arriving at dusk, we find two rooms, rather reasonably priced and with those unique French bathrooms again. My room has the shower and toilet all in one a plastic unit with a drain in the floor, and with a turning radius befitting a ballerina on tiptoes.

After a breakfast stroll through Châtellerault the next day, we drive and park next to the Vienne, the river flowing through the center of town. Our purpose is to try to catch a few of the rotund and (with any luck) plentiful scaled inhabitants of this swiftly flowing river. The local game warden is not to be seen (and we lack the local license and knowledge of how to obtain same). We set up the poles, and the bobbers float rapidly downstream. A few strings of seaweed are the only "catch of the day," and Patrick manages to lose my favorite rig, a beautiful small silver hand-painted fish. After an hour the fishermen (and I use that term rather lightly) abandon their quest. We pack up and head to La Merci Dieu, where my brother should have arrived by now.

Bonjour! My brother Christian, Anne, and Natascha arrive. After exiting their Twingo (as I glance with a bit of envy at their mode of transportation), my brother releases Jellie, Madame du Hamel's dog, who immediately dashes to the Twingo and starts to eat all the crumbs that are under Natascha's car seat. Natascha greets me, and we go for a walk to hunt *"gendarmes"* (policeman bugs). Why they have that name I don't know, but it is an amusing one. Our *"Petit Tour de France"* has come to an end, and it feels good to be here in our summer home for a week.

Seahorses & Squids
January 2002

Time to get up. 6:00 a.m. No pitter patter of feet to be heard yet. You thought I meant kids? Nope, I'm talking squirrels. I suppose the flat roof of the loft I live in is a temptation for little squirrel feet to use as a freeway off-ramp to their surrounding trees. I have been living in this loft in Oakland for six months now, having returned from France and Germany after the summer. When I first arrived, I slept in a motel and then the church again for a few days, and was ready to give up on living in the U.S. The senior pastor prayed with me, and then I found this place listed in the paper. The landlords were willing to accept me despite my ruined credit, and I was thankful to God for finally having a place of my own to call home again, after so many years.

After filling a large thermos with Earl Grey tea and packing up my camera, it's out the door and off we go, as the smell of the first acacia blossoms fills the morning air. Early January and already the acacias are blooming; it's a blessing to live in California.

I pick up Christian at 7:00 a.m. It's still dark (and the first time, to my knowledge, that he has gotten up early -- well, early for him -- by choice) for our trip to the Monterey Bay Aquarium. The Bay Bridge has almost no traffic, oh wonder of wonders. After traversing San Francisco, we reach beautiful Highway 1. Heavy fog engulfs the Pacific coast this morning, carrying the smell of the ocean inland. We decide to stop and take a walk on one of the coastline beaches. Winter driftwood is scattered on the beach, and as I balance on a long piece, equilibrium decides to stop working right next to a puddle, to Christian's amusement. One slightly wet foot. After strolling a bit trying to find a good piece of driftwood to carry home, we settle on leaving it to the beach and continue our drive. We stop in Davenport at the Whale City bakery, one of my favorite breakfast stops when heading south. After a vegetable omelet on Christian's part and a healthy bacon and eggs breakfast on mine, we continue. Since we are now in the vicinity of Santa Cruz, I introduce Christian to the cultural highlight of 107oink5 on the radio dial, KPIG from Freedom, California. It's a pleasant way to listen to some laid-back tunes in the morning. It replaced the old KFAT station, for those of you who remember the '70s. We pass by a bicycle shop in Santa Cruz; Big Bird greets us in front of the shop, promoting an economical mode of transportation.

A family tradition and mandatory next stop is the Giant Artichoke in Castroville. As luck would have it, there are winter-kissed artichokes for sale, the ones that have been nipped by a bit of frost and are slightly purple around the edges. Two ceramic artichokes, a bit smaller in size and functioning as salt and pepper shakers, warrant a purchase as well. After the obligatory family portrait standing in front of the Giant Artichoke, it's time to head to Monterey Bay.

The dunes of Sand City lie to the right of us, and a low fog still covers the entire Monterey Peninsula. After parking in Cannery Row, we walk down a few streets to the Monterey Bay Aquarium. In addition to their new jellies exhibit, which Christian has not seen, they have a special exhibit of seahorses. I didn't realize there were so many different varieties. They are graceful, delicate, and just mesmerizing -- what a marvel of creation. Luckily, the Aquarium is quiet today, so we

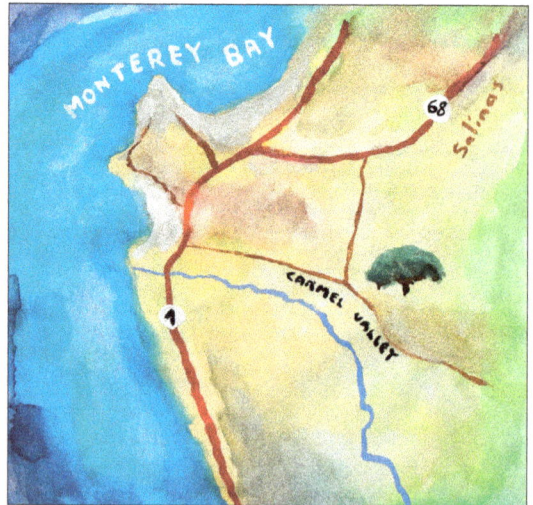

have a chance to slowly walk from tank to tank. Coming to the Outer Bay tank, I can't see any turtles or the sunfish at first, but we wait a while, and our patience is rewarded. The previous resident sunfish actually had to be lifted out by helicopter because of its size, but this one seems a bit, shall we say, less portly? He really does have a pretty easy environment for gaining weight here, with three squares or more per day. The green sea turtle, with a gentle slow motion of its flippers, glides past the top of the tank now, lest Mr. Sunfish should hog all the attention. In another tank, the leafy sea dragon, half plant and half creature in appearance, fascinates.

Coming downstairs, we walk through the glass door of the aviary. Cool air and fog greet us. The birds have become accustomed to their environment and to people; some are wading in the sand and surf, some have their heads tucked under their wings, and others are preening. In the lower part of the exhibit, where the simulated tide comes in and out, the shovelnose guitarfish and the sharks sluggishly let themselves drift about, while the sanddabs hide in the sand, only making their presence known once in a while with the closing of an eye or slight wiggle of a tailfin. "It's wintertime, stop bothering us."

Inside again, we pause at the basin of the rays, which are among my favorite creatures of the sea. Sometimes they will swim close enough so you can touch them, like a pet; their skin feels very soft and slippery. Today, however, word must have gotten around within the ray community that a school class is present, and the swim patterns are adjusted accordingly, so the rays stay just out of reach. Those little fingers are just a bit too active, and the rays know it.

Outside on the decks in back of the Aquarium, the fog has lifted, and Monterey Bay has turned from gray to blue. A very pretty seagull with dark plumage and a red beak decides to decorate a bench.

Back inside at the gift shop, Christian makes an amazing discovery, a giant stuffed-animal squid. Truly unique, it's four to five feet long including the tentacles. A must-have for any marine enthusiast. We purchase Mr.-To-Be-Named-Later, and then it's time to go; we still have a few miles ahead of us. After driving up Del Monte Boulevard for a bit, I panic and notice that my back-pack with camera is missing from the truck. Quickly turning around, we drive back down the hill as it occurs to me that we forgot to look at the new penguin exhibit. Next time, I guess. While I wait outside by the curb, Christian goes inside and manages to retrieve the backpack. Aquarium visitors are honest people.

The afternoon is late already and breakfast was a while back, so I am talked into honoring another family tradition: visiting KFC while on the road. I make the acquaintance of popcorn chicken; how they manage to stuff those chickens into little kernels is beyond me. The sun is now low on the horizon, so the drive is a bit more rapid than I was hoping it would be -- I'm trying to make it to Big Sur before sunset. As we approach Big Sur, lush green meadows are to the right and left of us as they always are at this time of year, dotted with cows, cows, and more cows; it reminds me of my trip to Normandy. The sun has almost set when we pull into the driveway of Ventana. We walk past the big oak barrel (which is cut in half and filled with water gently flowing over the sides onto the stones below) and through the doors to the outside deck. It's chilly, approaching cold, but the family tradition of drinking the world's best mai tai above the Pacific has to be honored. The last hope of daylight now fades and we take refuge next to the fire pit inside, which is stacked with logs and contains a roaring fire. It's hard to leave.

North on Route 1 back along the coast. With nightfall, the Big Sur area has now sunk into complete darkness, devoid of any lights.

Past the Carmel Highlands, I drive into Carmel Valley to cut over Los Laureles Grade and then over to Salinas. I have to work tomorrow, and Highway 101 will save us a little time. On the grade, we make a stop at one of my favorite viewpoints. In the daytime you can see the old oak trees on the hills across the way, and sometimes a fog bank hovering over Mid Valley. Tonight the stars beckon with their twinkling. We sit and gaze for a little while at this heavenly splendor. The chilly night air sends us back to the truck, and we cross over Los Laureles Grade. Salinas is visible in the distance. Since we named his brother Patrick's stuffed-animal turtle on a prior trip many years ago on the same route back from the Aquarium, I now suggest the name Mai Tai for Christian's giant squid. This finds approval. Its color certainly does the name justice, one would observe. During the remainder of the trip, we have a lot of theological discussions, and it is quite interesting to learn what Christian has been busy with at college. It's been a memorable day trip.

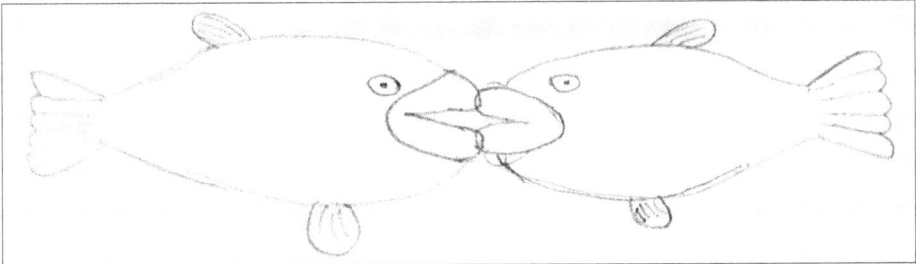

S lowly sitting up and looking out the window, I notice that a squirrel is busy scurrying through the treetops. I guess one has to follow this good example of an early riser and do likewise.

Airline ticket? Yup. Camera bag? Yup. Other bag? Yup. Ready to go. I walk to where the long driveway ends at the main road, and a taxi picks me up after I wave to make my presence known. Destination Oakland Airport. Too early for chit-chat, so we drive in silence. I notice that the meter clicks in 24 cent increments, an unusual number, perhaps attributable to the whim of an accountant, or to keep you on your toes.

At the Southwest Airlines terminal there is a very long line, two deep. Because of the new extra security precautions, I am asked to take off my shoes, along with other passengers selected at random. They include several children and an elderly woman, who for some strange reason I find hard to imagine as a threat to airline safety. My comment about preferring a pretty girl searching me instead of my male airport screener is met with a smirk. I guess a little humor is still appreciated in this business.

As the plane gets ready to make its final approach over Phoenix, a very colorful palette of aqua pool rectangles surrounded by green lawns, houses, and bordered by arid desert can be seen out the window. I step off the plane into 90° heat, amazing for early April. My friend Tom is parked at the curb and looking for me. He tells me he has had to circle the airport 15 times because the flight was delayed. I guess holding patterns apply to trucks too.

As we leave the airport via Interstate 17, saguaro cacti can be seen on both sides of our chosen route to the north. The interstate has amusing exit sign names, such as "Horse Thief" and "Bumblebee". One is inclined to assume a rather lengthy stay in the noonday sun was responsible for the aforementioned titles. After a long stretch broken up by a pit stop for fuel, we come to the northern Arizona city of Flagstaff. The terrain is mountainous. An old train and railway station conjure up images of the building of the railroads across this great land.

After shopping for groceries, we head for the Grand Canyon, our intended destination tonight. Aspen and Ponderosa pine dot this high terrain. It's getting toward dusk, and we are still a ways from the canyon. Tom wants to keep driving, but I talk him out of it for three very good reasons, the first being that a campsite has just come up in front of us; the second, I'm hungry; and the third, it's no fun pitching camp in the dark. The campsite turns out to be based upon the "Flintstones" motif. It has bright, colorful rock walls, complete with a "prehistoric" car with wheels made out of rock, true to the cartoon. After registering with Wilma (or is it Betty?), we set up camp. Reason number three fulfills itself now, too, and with the aid of a flashlight Tom sets up the tents, while I start dinner. A brisk breeze has given a chill to the evening, but the stove's flickering flame fights on bravely. I don't know about you, dear reader, but despite decades of camping experience and proficiency at making lists, I still always manage to forget at least one item, and thus our sizzling pork chops get a double dose of pepper, due to the absence of salt. They sure taste good, though, and they stick to the ribs as the night air gets even colder. Bedtime, and let's hope Dino and his dinosaur friends aren't nocturnal.

After a hearty breakfast in the Flintstones coffee shop we pack up, but not before posing and taking pictures with the rock wheel car. At the end of a short drive we come to Grand Canyon National Park. After being greeted by the park ranger, we book a site near the South Rim and set up camp. The higher altitude is quite a bit cooler than the desert, but the sun is up and the chill is gone.

Our camp for the next two nights set up, we drive over to the parking lot near the lodge. A train still comes right into the Canyon Station here, a very nice alternative to driving if you plan way ahead for a leisurely trip. We walk past the visitor parking lot and over to the edge of the Grand Canyon. You can look at all the photographs and postcards you want, but they cannot match the real thing. I remember a book I read as a kid called "Mystery at Rustler's Fort," which took place down at the bottom of the canyon, and so I suggest hiking down to check it out, grossly misjudging the elevation. Tom reminds me that we only have two days here, which would barely be enough time to climb down and then back up. I'm convinced, and we then decide to hike along the rim trail. I can't stop marveling at the grandeur of the canyon. Every bend brings new views and rock formations in the most spectacular shades of color. The fact that we hear languages from every part of the world confirms that this is one of the most popular national parks in America. After a long hike with water and photo stops along the way, we head back to camp for lunch and a nap. A raven is sitting on the clothesline we have put up between two trees, and we also find a note on the picnic table prohibiting hanging of same. Sorry, Mr. Raven, it looks like a ranger (who perhaps normally resides at a desk), in describing our clothesline as a potential hazard for birds, has thus deprived you of a place to perch to watch our picnic table for leftovers. Take it up with the pencil-pusher.

The afternoon shadows appear as we head over to the lodge, the western side this time. The rocks start to glow in warm colors as the sun begins to set. The stillness and vastness of the Grand Canyon leave a lasting impression. I don't recall what we had for dinner that night, and since Tom is on the road in an 18-wheeler somewhere right now, he is not available to jog my memory; and so, dear reader, I must apologize for depriving you of the evening's menu.

I do remember bacon, eggs, and thinly sliced potatoes for breakfast, though, along with some good hot coffee. There is nothing like the smell of bacon and coffee as you shake off the early morning chills. Our destination today is Desert View, which lies to the east of the South Rim of the canyon. We arrive at a tower built in intricate layers of stone. I guess you can't go anywhere without getting hit up for an admission charge, but after paying this one, it proves well worth it as we climb to the top. The inside of the tower is decorated with beautiful Hopi Indian (or "Native American," as I am always corrected by my sons) drawings depicting their life and the animals that are part of their culture. The sometimes simple, often eloquent drawings pay tribute to the Hopi way of life, be it the hunt for buffalo or the mending of tents. When we step outside onto the terrace next to the stone staircase, a vast, expansive view lies before us. In the far distance below, a tiny bluish turquoise piece of the Colorado River can be seen. A low but scattered layer of clouds lets the sun play with shadows on the rock formations below. On the way back to camp we see a few ravens taking care of their assigned duty as scavengers on the side of the road. I suggest to Tom we should inform "our" raven, who has been prohibited from sitting on our clothesline, that he is missing out on a meal here that his selfish compatriots are not sharing.

In the late afternoon we walk to the rim of the canyon again, but this time we take the shuttle bus to the last stop on the route, the westernmost point of the canyon, which is called Hermit's Rest. Our bus driver points out Alligator Rock, a formation that does its name justice.

An older gentleman suggests: "Man, them Injuns did a lot of diggin,'" after a glimpse out the bus window. The other passengers are amused, although his wife seems a bit embarrassed. After a short stop, we backtrack to Navajo Point and set up our cameras, waiting for the sunset.

Clouds gather, and it is absolutely still again. There are only a few folks here, as it is getting towards dusk. All of a sudden, I see a multitude of shadows moving over the lower portions of the vast canyon. Quickly borrowing Tom's binoculars, I see what they are: condors, the birds with the largest wingspan in the world. Their graceful flight is effortless as they let the wind currents carry them, sometimes below and sometimes above us. God made these birds to live here. The deep hues of blue and purple and the far-off Colorado River add an unforgettable backdrop. Tom has to drag me away -- I can't get enough of watching the condors.

The sky is almost black, and the evening chill is all around as we stand in the roadway along with a few other stragglers, waiting for the last shuttle bus. The headlights appear, and everyone is glad to get on the bus and head back. You don't want to be stranded out here at night. After a good stiff drink in the lodge to warm up the bones, we head back to camp for dinner and a good night's rest.

The next morning, after we pack up, our route takes us out of Grand Canyon National Park and through the Painted Desert. Tom has never been to Monument Valley, and he asks me if I'm up for taking a detour. Talks me into it easily. The Painted Desert deserves its name: the sand comes in all shades and colors, a beautiful contrast to the lonely blacktop highway. After a while we come through a town called Tuba City, named by the musically inclined, no doubt. I'm sorry to report that no tuba sounds were heard to give it credence, though.

We enter Monument Valley. It almost seems like a moon landscape, with vast stretches of flat land with giant red rock formations jutting up out of the ground. Stopping for a "Kodak Moment," I photograph a brown and white mustang (no, not the car), a picture postcard to be sure. On both sides of the straight road leading to the horizon, cattle graze, completing the idyllic western landscape. The wind has picked up a bit, and Tom keeps talking about a storm coming. After a while we come to Four Corners, named for the four states that meet here, and we cross the border into Utah. After a short pit stop in the town of Mexican Hat, we continue on to the landmark that gave the town its name and the tourists their bumper stickers: a large rock precariously balanced on a thin pointed rock, much as a juggler would balance a plate on a stick. The resemblance to a *sombrero* is appropriate. Tom is now constantly bugging me about the approaching sandstorm, which is driving me nuts. First of all, coming from California where we have earthquakes, this should be a minor irritation; secondly, if it gets too strong, we can always pull over and wait or take a nap; and lastly, there is nothing we can do about it anyway. But no: storm's a-comin', storm's a-comin', storm's a-comin'.

Finally, the sandstorm does arrive, with strong gusty winds blowing the tumbleweeds across the highway. It's a fascinating and beautiful sight. We continue driving through it, but does that stop Tom from talking about the sandstorm? No, it doesn't. Finally, I manage to distract him. Then the storm subsides, and we pull over. I step outside to take a few photos of the bright red soil, which the light rain has now turned into bright red mud. The color is incredibly intense, and the air has an unbelievably fresh smell to it. In this harsh environment, what little lives here is now storing the precious drops of rain for future survival.

After another long stretch of road southbound, we stop at the

Canyon de Chelli National Monument. The rain is still sprinkling off and on, so we can't visit the famous caves carved into the rock walls, but a short stop at the visitor center is a welcome break. Numerous large-scale photographs, some with people in them, give you an idea of the immensity of the rock and the caves. A silver-smith is working near the entrance of the center, making his beautiful jewelry in the typical Navajo turquoise and silver. One of the artifacts hanging on the wall stands out: this traditional Indian rug not only has the usual animals and dwellings depicted on it, but also includes a pickup truck. I am very amused.

Nightfall is approaching, and I'm having a hard time getting Tom to stop driving and find a motel. We finally stop in the town of Show Low -- although the exact details escape me, it was named for some type of poker game. We find a Motel 6 and I get a room from the clerk. Apparently Tom is dissatisfied with a non-smoking room and stubbornly decides to spend the night sleeping in the truck. He must have forgotten that I mentioned to him before our trip that I have a hard time with cigarette smoke. Maybe all the miles, and sleeping on the ground, have taken their toll on both the stubborn mules. I decide to walk into town and have dinner at a western steak house. On the way back I get lost, and have to walk a few extra miles until I finally find the motel again.

Next morning, showered and shaved, I pour out some fresh coffee and walk over to the truck to offer Tom a cup. With a grunt it is declined. Oh well, suit yourself. I pack up my stuff and we start heading towards Phoenix. As we drive through the mountains and the elevation gets higher, we suddenly see snow on the pines. Snow in Arizona? The winding mountain road with its beautiful scenery must be having a positive effect on Tom, for the grumbling stops and he holds forth a verbal olive branch, which I accept. A few sparse words are exchanged. After reaching the lower elevations, we stop for a large breakfast.

In the flat desert again, saguaros and ocotillos surround us. A few small cacti are even in bloom. Reaching the outskirts of Phoenix, we drive along miles and miles of straight road, with tacky mobile home sales lots and car dealerships flanking the road. Some parts of the road are landscaped with long rows of blooming trees, though, and those are very picturesque.

We find another Motel 6 near the airport, and I check in. I try two rooms, but they both smell like cheap car air freshener. Out of funds and patience, I settle for a room, since it's close to the airport.

Tom tells me he has heard a lot of good things about the Desert Botanical Garden, a highlight of Phoenix, so we decide on a visit.

Acres and acres of landscaped yet natural-looking desert greet us. You can see all types of cacti, with many in bloom. There is a meadow of tall grass, with hundreds and hundreds of flowers in every shade of red, yellow, orange and white: spring in all its splendor. I take a photo for reference, which I will use to later paint a Monet-like watercolor. There is a special exhibit, scattered all around the garden, of giant wooden insects: a praying mantis hiding behind a saguaro, ants walking the trails, a dragonfly hovering. These artistic creations blend in well despite their size, and are rather whimsical. A few agaves are in bloom, and the sweet scent of a honey-acacia permeates another section of the garden. One segment is dubbed the Hummingbird and Butterfly Garden. In a large tent, hundreds of butterflies drink the nectar of flowers, or come to sit on you. Simply delightful.

The afternoon is getting late and we head back to the motel. I suggest to Tom that he spend the night, but he wants to get home despite the long drive still ahead. Adios! Drive safely. A colorful trip, amigo!

The orange-and-gold Southwest Airlines plane takes me home to Oakland the next day, and my son Patrick picks me up. My red poppies are blooming in the planter box in front of my loft! It's chili dogs for lunch and a little chitchat about the trip. Got you a present, too: airline peanuts!

McFlurry at the Grande Arche
Summer 2002

Early afternoon: Patrick has just picked me up at home and is taking me to the airport. I remind him that he still has to clean the camping stove sitting outside on the porch, forlorn, lonely and neglected after our trip to Big Sur. He promises to do so. As we drive down 101, he is constantly switching radio stations, doing a good job of driving his father nuts. Last words of advice about keeping the house in order while I am in Germany get the response, "Don't worry, the landlord won't have to call 911 too often." Ah, nothing like a little reassurance. "Goodbye, please don't forget to water the tomatoes."

A few hours into the flight as I get up to go to the rest room, my seat neighbor asks me: "Gonna get out?" An amusing proposition at this altitude.

CDG, the other Parisian airport, comes into view after a good flight. The clouds are gleaming silver in the afternoon light. After claiming my gray Twingo (later to be named "Regenwolke" [rain cloud] by my god-daughter) at the Renault rental car center, I stop to get gas and then study my printouts and maps, trying to find the bargain 3-star hotel I have booked on the internet. After navigating through Paris, I manage to find it, and an underground garage is nearby for Regenwolke too. I enter the lobby with my suitcases, and the clerk acknowledges my reservation and gives me my room key. The lobby is a little shabby, but I ignore that fact. After lumbering up several flight of tall stairs I find my room. Lovely! About the size of a closet and the shower is in the same plastic booth as the toilet. Efficiency if I ever saw it. The "window" looks out on a charming light shaft, which has the added advantage that it enhances the noise coming from nearby buildings. As I sag into the U-shaped bed, resting my head on the "sausage" pillow, I marvel at the 3-star rating. I venture to presume that the reviewer knocked his head on a low overhang on the way up here, and saw triple in regard to stars. Venturing downstairs to go out for dinner, I notice the desk clerk shift has changed. At my rather polite question phrased in my best French inquiring as to the current time, Madame apparently feels her hard work of doing nothing has been disrupted by this unruly guest, and points to a clock across the lobby without a word. I guess this is what makes Americans take the next flight out. I for one will not be intimidated quite yet, for dinner beckons.

After walking along a few streets, I find a marvelous restaurant. Its specialty is "*moules et frites*" or mussels and French fries, if you must know. The aroma of the steaming mussels in broth coming from the iron pot is mouth-watering. There is plenty of bread for dipping, and the *frites* are perfectly done. The additional tall glass of beer is a perfect complement. The world is all right again; forgotten are the "3 stars" and the pondered possibility of vindictive letters to the hotel association.

Breakfast the next morning is in the hotel basement, which has the appearance of a cave. *Bon!* A *café au lait* that comes in a huge cup and the *croissants* are scrumdideliumptious (to borrow a phrase from one of my favorite authors), too. There is a slight drizzle as I exit the hotel to try to find a department store selling umbrellas. As in years before, having forgotten that the sun doesn't shine here all the time like at home in California, I once again will subsidize the French economy. Said purchase is briefly delayed, however, in the form of a fresh apple tart from a *pâtisserie* that has lured me in with its smell. Mission accomplished. Afterwards, a blue umbrella it is. I run into two fellow tourists, a mother and daughter from Canada who, as it turns out, are headed to the Notre Dame as am I. We comment on the "awful" weather, reaching the side entrance door at a brisk pace, trying to escape the increasing Paris rain. The early hour and bad weather have kept the hordes away. It's a long and musty climb up the steep stone steps to the top. Once outside, the beautiful cityscape of Paris unfolds under gray skies. The golden glow of a steeple can be seen in the distance, and below the railing the oxidized green rooftops repel a barrage of raindrops. The famous gargoyles gaze over the city from their posts. I manage to take a few pictures before I drop one of my cameras, putting it out of commission for the rest of the trip. After exchanging hotel recommendations, or in my case places to avoid, I part ways with my Canadian acquaintances.

The next stop is the Centre Pompidou, a place I have visited twice before. The building resembles an oil refinery but houses modern art. It is on the list of attractions in the "Museum Pass" I purchased at a *Métro* Station. One of the guards tells me I have to check my back-pack, camera and umbrella to go upstairs, so I opt to descend to the less restrictive lower level, where there is an exhibit of Renault cars. The Avantime is the eye-catcher: a unique new car with a glass roof stretching from front to back; one could envision this car as a fish tank. It's remarkable -- French engineering at its best in the tradition of the Concorde, once again. After buying a book on gardens for an architect friend of mine, I exit the center in search of lunch. A small *bistro* with a very friendly waiter is found a few blocks away. In one corner, a dog is lying under a table, patiently awaiting scraps. It's nice to see this tolerant attitude towards dogs. My "*croque madame*" and a *café* afterwards make for a pleasant light lunch. *Monsieur chien* did receive a small scrap, in case you must know.

Afterwards, I take a stroll across one of the bridges of the Seine. It's a lot of fun watching the barges, laden with their various cargoes, pass underneath. Some travel very swiftly, others just putter along. Occasionally, the captain or a deckhand waves back as I wave to them. Bicycles and sometimes even small cars sit at the end of the long barges to provide transport for the barge dwellers' land visits. Not only are the barges self-contained homes, but an important form of commercial transport. Also gliding underneath the Pont Neuf are the "*batobusses,*" the sometimes open, sometimes covered sightseeing boats full to the brim with tourists enjoying the water-level view of this great city at this time of year. Reluctantly, I leave the bridge to go back to my hotel and check out.

I had only planned to stay one night in Paris, but since my brother Christian's plans have changed, I am here for another two days before driving south with him. My experience in the "3-star" hotel has convinced me to seek accommodations away from Paris, and so I start heading out, but get lost taking the smaller secondary roads. The gray suburbs with their massive concrete slab apartment buildings on the outskirts of the city are a pretty depressing sight. I continue to the smaller towns. It is getting toward evening already, and my stops at a few places to find lodging for the night are unsuccessful. They are always "*complet*". I guess because it is July and the height of the tourist season. One "*non*" at a small country inn is especially disappointing as the smells coming from the kitchen have a Pied Piper effect. Exasperated, I drive on, tired and jet-lagged. Finally, near dusk, I come to Meaux, a town which I passed through a few years back. Next to the Marne river quietly flowing along, I find a medium-sized hotel with a decent room. The clerk looks me over a few times and wonders why I look so exhausted. He then recommends a nearby restaurant for dinner. After showering and unpacking, I make my way through the night to same. It is also next to the river. The smiling waiter makes a suggestion of sauerkraut surrounded by a multitude of different sausages, and a good beer to go along with it. It's a sumptuous meal, although not exactly what one thinks of as French cuisine, but more along the line of items consumed in my country. The only distractionis a couple of Americans at a table across the room

116

conversing at TV commercial volume. My guess is: lawyers. Strangely enough, I can hear even them better than the French couple at the table next to me. The waiter brings the ice cream, and the loud couple is forgotten as my attention is refocused.

The next morning, blue sky greets the day, and since I have a little free time after breakfast before checkout, I decide to take a stroll through Meaux. It's a picturesque small town with a castle rising in its middle. Climbing up the narrow alleys, I see workmen restoring some of the old castle wall. I find a few batteries for my CD player and continue my morning stroll. There is a flower shop on one corner, and the fragrance of fresh cut flowers fills the air. Another shop has fruit specialties in grand display, as well as a variety of jars of homemade preserves and jams. After the purchase of a jar of jam and a little wine and some bread to go along with it, I walk back to the hotel. Checked out and packed, it's time for some tunes in my little Twingo, as I drive along the Marne.

I have decided, albeit somewhat reluctantly, to spend the last night in Paris once again, as my brother Christian will be arriving tomorrow at the Gare du Nord. Before being swallowed up by the big city again, it's time to take in a little countryside. I come by the small town of Claye-Souilly, where I stayed with my sons Christian and Patrick a few years back, on our last night before flying back to the U.S. It's really nice to see it again, and I still remember the delicious *crèpes* we ate there, across the street from the hotel we stayed at, and Patrick spinning a basketball on his finger to the delight of a French kid. I stop at the hotel and ask for a room, but unfortunately they are also full, even for a returning customer. It's now early afternoon and I start to worry about a repeat of yesterday. Making my way into Paris I stop at an IBIS, one of the reasonable chain hotels. "*Complet.*" However, the friendly receptionist offers to call another IBIS for me to check availability, and tells me I'm in luck, there is one room left. I'm very grateful for her help. Arriving at the second IBIS after getting lost several times, I try to check in, but it takes three explanations to convince the girl that the other IBIS has reserved a room for me here. Finally, she finds it, and is also nice enough to give me one of the scarce parking spots in the garage, a favor I later repay with a bag of roasted almonds. Thank you, God, for sending this weary traveler nice people.

After bringing my bags up to the room, I make my way to La Villette, the "Science City" surrounded by vast expanses of parks. Crossing over a canal via a bridge, I notice a funny sign next to the canal: Boat Parking, 6 Hours. I wonder if the meter maids (I presume they are seaworthy) really give out tickets for nautical infractions. Inside one of the science buildings is an exhibit about train history. I watch a remarkable film in which a TGV (a high-speed French train) reaches 525km, a milestone in railroad history. In the film you can clearly see the thrill on the faces of the conductor, the engineers, and the cameramen, as the train breaks the speed record. Heading back outside shortly before closing time, I see a group of young men playing soccer. One of them makes a heroic save of the ball from going into the canal.

I go back to the hotel, then venture out on an evening stroll to encourage a proper dinner appetite (what else do you do in France except eat?). I see a very different Paris from what the tour books depict; this is an ethnically diverse neighborhood, and you can tell people actually live here. Many restaurants from regions of the former French colonies line both sides of the main street, tempting the stroller with their various delicacies and aromas. It's really interesting to get this different perspective of the "real" Paris. After winding my way through a few side streets, I come back to the long canal that leads to La Villette. It's a lovely warm evening, and every couple of dozen yards people are playing *boules*, one of the national pastimes. There are arguments, lively discussions and laughter as the participants measure which of the heavy lead balls come closest to the little wooden one. Some of the expert players can bounce away the other players' *boules* with pinpoint accuracy. I watch a few games, then continue my stroll along the canal. Across on the other side a mother and her young daughter are visible through the window of an apartment building. The little girl waves to me and I wave back. At the end of the canal near a railroad bridge, I turn up a side street that leads back to the hotel. There are loud noises coming from the area of La Villette, similar to what you hear from boom boxes that are popular in cars, but with greater resonance. Must be dance night.

The restaurant lobby is starting to gather its guests. An amusing pictogram sign of a suitcase with a red circle around it and a red line through it on my table advises one to keep an eye on one's belongings, although the restaurant strikes me as quite civil. A few tables around me are occupied by single businessmen ordering their dinner. Some look tired, some are alone, and the pleasant waitress manages to make them all relax and smile while taking their order. After a friendly "*bonjour*" from her at my table I settle for steak and *frites*.

The next morning, well nourished by a buffet breakfast, I head out the door to explore some more of Paris. The skies are overcast but it is dry. After a brisk walk I find a *Métro* station. Handing the station agent a twenty EURO note to buy tickets, I am reprimanded and sent to a bank to get change. A few blocks away, I spot one with a policeman and his dog in front of it. I enter a heavy glass door which shuts and locks behind me. Then I press a button and the second glass door opens. Then after getting change, the same procedure once again. Must be quite a rough neighborhood, I think to myself, as the policeman looks me up and down suspiciously upon my exit. His dog, however, refrains from such blatant visual scrutinizing. I think it better not to ask him if he is perhaps Inspector Clouseau. Mission accomplished, I go back to get my *Métro* tickets. This time *Madame* is more forthcoming.

Transferring a few times among the many *Métro* lines, I exit at the station nearest to Parc André Citroën. A school class walks by, their busy teachers keeping them all in order. It looks like a field trip; the kids are excited and goofing off. Parc André Citroën used to be a Citroën factory, but then was abandoned and fell into decay. It is now a huge park with fountains and waterfalls and beds upon beds of flowers and plants. Gigantic greenhouses filled with large trees and subtropical plants sit at one end of the park. Large containers of oleander are sitting outside for the summer -- and to think they are just ordinary freeway dividers in California! After walking the entire circumference of the park, I make my way back to the *Métro* for one last short visit to one to my favorite spots in Paris, La Défense.

Arriving at the underground station, a few late commuters flank me left and right as they head to their offices. I make a quick stop in one of the department stores to buy some cleaning products for my Twingo. As I try to enter the store, a security guard stops me and points me to a table where I have to seal my backpack in a plastic bag by means of a machine resembling a soldering iron before bringing it into the store. I guess there is great faith in the honesty of the clientele here.

For the viewing benefit of my sons upon my return, I then stop at the fine dining establishment of McDonald's to purchase a McFlurry, with which I then ask to be photographed sitting on the steps leading up to the "Grand Arche" (the modern Arc de Triomphe), much to the bemusement of the Parisian office worker. A slight drizzle is in the air, but the high gray clouds still leave good visibility of this expansive, breathtaking tableau of glass, steel, and concrete. My sister-in-law once told me she thought this place was cold, but I marvel at the form, color, and creativity of the buildings surrounding the vast open space, although it could use some plants, perhaps. In a tent set up near the middle of the open space, next to a multicolored tiled basin filled with water, a band from Cuba is playing a lunchtime gig. The music attracts tourists and office workers alike, and pretty soon lots of people are swaying or dancing to the sound of percussion and a great horn section. You can feel summer has arrived, and the city is ready for some fun. After the musicians stop playing and receive much applause, I leave to make my photographic rounds of La Défense.

I only go a few stops with the *Métro* this time, getting off near the Champs-Elysées to take a look at the Arc de Triomphe. As I come out of the passage, the rain starts again, and I dash from tree to tree to escape it, but then give up my plans to climb to the top of the Arc this year, as the rain gets heavier and heavier. Too bad, that spot is a real special one for looking down at the circling cars. Sniff, sniff. Back down below, the *Métro* trains are starting to fill up again with early afternoon commuters on their way home. Arriving back at my hotel, I pick up my Twingo Regenwolke from the garage (its name certainly described this day). I study my map and head for the Gare du Nord to claim my brother, who is arriving by TGV from Germany via Belgium. Sure enough, there he is, can't really miss two meters and seven centimeters. It's so nice to see him again after a year. The late afternoon commute traffic has started, and the rains are torrential, not to mention that it's Friday. Can't get any worse. I play navigator this time, and after finally reaching the outskirts of Paris, the *Autoroute* south greets us. La Merci Dieu, here we come!

Part 1: Glass and Shower Spout

I wander into my local hardware store this morning, carrying two pieces of glass that are broken off at the edges due to, shall we put it, a lack of proper attention. My aim is to have them cut a size smaller, thus rendering them useful for again filling photo frames. I have seen someone cut a piece of glass here before, so I figure I am in good hands.

After inquiring of one of the workers if this "downsizing" might be possible, I am told yes. My expert glass cutter, Jim I believe is his name, proceeds to take the first piece of glass and fit it on the glass cutter, a process commented upon by one of his compatriots named Steve, who estimates this will cost me a mere $100. Jim thinks this a bit pricey, and Steve starts to wonder if Jim is capable of cutting glass, asking if he has received his proper dose of Geritol at the old folks' home. And so it continues. Stan and Ollie in action. I indeed receive two pieces of glass properly cut to size, which Steve proceeds to wrap in brown paper. Jim questions him as to whether he is wrapping a Christmas present, noticing Steve's patience and dexterity, and suggests that perhaps a bow is in order too. I am told there is no charge, and find inscribed upon the package: "With Love, Steve and Jim". I hand them two dollar bills: "Buy yourself a soda, and thank you for the morning's entertainment, gentlemen."

Two pieces of glass under my arm, I am, however, unsuccessful at purchasing a replacement shower spout from Jim and Steve. The spout failed to function properly this morning, and I disassembled it and brought it with me. I am given directions to two other hardware stores somewhat nearby, and at the second one I find success in obtaining a new spout, something my shower is eagerly awaiting now. As I receive my sales slip, I am told to go through a door, to another office to pay for the spout and where I will be given a receipt as well. As I proceed to pay, I can't help but notice a clock on the wall in the shape of a toilet seat. I will refrain from puns here, and believe I am safe to assume that this type of clock will probably not grace most homes.

Part 2: Dog Days

I think it was dog day today.

Having parked my truck in the underground garage at the supermarket, which grants one a two-hour window of opportunity (with a purchase upstairs, if you want to be correct about it), I emerge from the garage to take a walk along the nearby park. Spring is in the air, and magnolia leaves are trying to outnumber magnolia blossoms on the trees. The scales seem to be tipped in favor of the leaves -- I see an abundance of blossoms on the ground below. Fruit trees are sprouting their whites, pinks, and reds early, as it has been such a dry, warm, almost non-existent winter here in Northern California.

As the park ends, I walk along the main road. Mailboxes line the street at various intervals; one has the flap down and is stuffed to the gills with mail, beckoning the owner to retrieve and relieve. A tall thicket of bamboo runs along the fence of one yard, inhibiting a view. The next house has a sign on the side gate: "Dog behind fence". Why, thank you for informing us of this supposed fact. I guess it's good the dog is not in front of or on top of the fence. I question the validity of the statement, however, as I do not hear barking, whining, sniffing, or other dog-related sounds. The sign is a bit more diplomatic than one I saw some years ago though; it noted: "Never mind the dog, beware of the owner".

As I round the corner of the next street, I see a rosemary bush in full bloom. I always have to stop when I see a rosemary bush to rub its leaves between my fingers and inhale the aroma that I always associate with culinary adventures. There is a car parked on the side street with a bumper sticker that says: "Wag more, bark less". Transposed to the human realm, this seems like excellent advice to me.

Having made the small loop back to the main street, I pass a group of school children being led by their teachers. Surprisingly, they are walking almost two-by-two in an orderly fashion. Unusual behavior for children. Crossing over to the other side of the street -- OK, I admit jay-walking -- I pass a chocolate and candy store. In the window I see a ceramic cookie jar in the shape of a dog. A beautiful jar, but with a prohibitive price tag which I notice as I enter the store from the other side of the window. I do believe this jar could hold three to four pack-ages of cookies, unless you have a canine who insists it be filled with his or her treats instead of cookies.

As I enter one of the Peet's coffee stores I frequent, I see a dog "regular" outside, by the name of Muffy, who despite petite stature and failing eyesight nonetheless won't miss a crumb that falls to the ground. Today she is being held in her owner's arms. Perhaps a better aerial perspective of potential treats.

A medium caffe latte later, having been questioned as to what kind of milk it should include, to which I always respond, "Real milk," I exit via the front door and sit on the bench outside for a bit. One of these days, I will have them trained as to what "real milk" is. A woman is sitting next to me with her toddler who has a big smile and holds a small bowl of goldfish snacks. A very good reason to smile, I tend to agree. Another dog owner walks by. The dog, small in stature, is wearing a down vest. Now, I don't speak dog, but I presume this indignity is not easily borne when encountering other four-footed friends. Silly humans. The toddler has managed to eat some of his goldfish, and the mom has prevented several potential spills. She seems apologetic for the activity, but I just smile, no problem here. Soon, a woman

walks by carrying her dog in her arms. I turn to the mom on the bench and I start laughing as I point out the fact that the woman and the dog seem to have the same hairdo. She laughs too, as she watches the little white fluffy dog and her whitehaired owner disappearing down the street.

OK, time to go and retrieve my truck before the chalk-wielding patrol gets too giddy about the approaching two-hour limit. Although I have no qualms about parking in the garage, I nonetheless ascend the non-working escalator (which is almost always out of order). A gourmet purchase today: two Healthy Choice frozen dinners, a box of cat food, and today's paper. As there are long lines, I opt for the, to me, hated electronic check-out counter. One of the regular employees assists me to tame the unruly beast and to retrieve change returned from its mysterious innards.

Arriving home and parking in the alley, I see the cleaned-up neighboring yard that used to contain three chihuahuas, the most annoying little barking rats I have ever encountered. The memory sends shudders down my back. I suspect this last sentence has roused the ire of chihuahuas (and their owners) everywhere, but so be it! I will just have to guard my ankles.

One day later: it seems that yesterday's "dog day" has a small addition today. Walking up to OSH to purchase a tomato cage, I am verbally assaulted through the crack of a window by a pint-sized would-be dog, which goes into further hysterics as I approach the window to say hello. I read the name tag, which says Suzie, and call her name. This results in a halt to the frenzied barking, twitching ears, and a look of "Hey -- how come you know my name?"

I depart to collect my tomato cage. I hope it will be a warm summer, unlike the past two years, which produced almost no tomatoes, much to the dismay of local gardening enthusiasts. One green colored tomato cage later, I head over to Berkeley Bowl to purchase some salmon (they have really good salmon) and some asparagus and red potatoes to keep it company. I thought I was done with dogs, but no, what do I see at the check-out counter? A dog magazine. The headline asks, "Is your dog too fat?" As I ponder this dilemma, which may plague the occasional dog owner, I am asked if my preference is paper or plastic. No easy answers today, it seems.

Addendum to Dog Days: My faithful old truck is having problems with the recently replaced engine computer, as the idle speed is still too high and the engine is revving too high during normal operation as well. I decide to drop it off down the street with my mechanic, who is very good at finding and fixing stuff. He promises to replace the computer once again. Luckily it is still under warranty -- the computer, not my 24-year-old truck. Having retrieved my house key from the key ring that holds the truck keys, I head up the street. Being a creature of routine, I normally walk the same streets to head back home, but this time I take an alternate one, don't know why. Thus I have the privilege not only to see many fruit trees in bloom, the California spring sun helping their endeavors to stretch and unfold, but I also go by a yard where I spot a sign: "Possibly dangerous dog". Now, this makes one ponder. Do I bring a sausage next time to appease any possible malevolence? Will one get growled at on Tuesdays? Barked at on Thursdays? Many possibilities. I wonder if the owner is aware of the dilemmas he is creating, or the dog, for that matter. All remains calm on this Wednesday, however, and the inhabitant is neither to be heard nor seen. Nonetheless, this has my full attention and thought all the way back to the house.

Finally some rain relief. It's been such a wet March this year. I'm short a few grocery items and I also want to find some fig jam as an Easter present for my neighbors, as they like it so much, so it's off to the Village to the grocery store. Unfortunately, I can't find any jam, so I will have to try another place I know later. I'm going to pass on coffee today, too, since I have a bit of heartburn. Going back to the car, I pass a woman sitting outside the coffee shop holding her chihuahua. Will these dog-intrusions never end? Or am I innundated with dogs? My cat Calvin always sniffs my hand after I have petted one with what I deem an expression of polite yet somewhat reluctant interest. But

I digress. Said chihuahua has on a camouflage army uniform. I can barely stifle a laugh, although I'm guarding my ankles after my prior statement. No doubt this is the terror of the neighborhood, with those fierce carnivorous fangs ready to rip into unsuspecting flesh. We do not make eye contact as I bravely walk straight by.

Part 3: Easter

My mother used to rub Easter eggs with bacon fat after coloring them, which made them take on a bright shine and added to the intensity of the colors. However, this had the downside effect that when they were hidden in the garden or around the house, they were easily and joyously discovered by the St. Bernards my parents had. An advance scouting party, if you will.

This year, despite the fact that I live alone, I decide to try the same for my cat Calvin. Not only do I color a few eggs, but I draw a cat face on his egg, and eggs with my sons' faces and their girlfriends' faces on them (photos of which I transmit electronically later). I must say that after I rub Calvin's egg with a slice of bacon he is more than intrigued with the egg, although at a loss as to how something that smells so good can be devoured in a proper manner, as the size is intimidating. I admit it, I end up eating his egg.

Part 4: At the Pond

Another morning outing to the park. Some of my French bread has become rather stale, and although I tend to use it to make bread crumbs for cooking, I figure I have enough to share with some of the feathered citizens residing in a nearby pond. Parking in my usual underground supermarket parking lot, peering left and right to make sure the chalker of tires is nowhere to be seen, I make my exit and walk past the playground to the pond. I start to break the bread into small pieces and observe a mother and her small child standing a bit away from me. Between us is a large sign regulating waterfowl on this pond. The mother is explaining the ecological dos and don'ts written on the sign: natural habitats, no feeding, etc., etc. Meanwhile, I'm feeding the approaching ducks and geese, who are delightedly squabbling over their unexpected breakfast. The kid is confused, looking simultaneously at me, the obvious law-breaker, and listening to what the mother is reading on the sign. To answer his perplexed look and at the same time smiling at the mom, I respond that bread is OK. After all, I'm not feeding Twinkies and Ding-Dongs, but a staple that has been consumed by generations of ducks, before the sign planters entered our present world. The squabble over the bread on the surface of the pond continues, the faster ducks prevailing. To my surprise, several turtles appear and start to nibble at the bread. Unfortunately, they are brutishly overrun by several of the large geese. Even an attempt to distribute the bread a bit further out proves futile, as, after all, a turtle is a turtle and thus slow, and no match for a goose or bread-obsessed duck.

One last dog; well, sort of. Making my way around the park to retrieve my vehicle, I encounter what looks like a fox being walked on a leash. I remark to the owner that it is quite unusual to see a fox on a leash, but she educates me that this is a breed of dog resembling a fox. It's

a good thing we don't reside in the United Kingdom where this fine specimen might be mistaken for a fox and pursued in a foxhunt. After I pet Mr. Fox, who appears a bit skittish, we part ways.

I stand corrected; yet one *more* dog: Strolling through the Sunday Farmer's Market after service, enjoying samples of orange-honey, European-style butter, and orange-flavored non-dairy ice cream, I

pass by a fluffy looking dog that I reach down to pet, commenting to the owner what a fine specimen this is. She tells me it's a Golden-doodle, which I think must be a joke, but she informs me it's not, it's a mix between a Golden Retriever and a Poodle. Sounds like a cookie to me, though.

Reviews:

Matthias Leue takes you on a journey with him through each of his delightful travel stories. His keen photographer's eye and easygoing nature are evident in every word he has written to share his adventures with you. He not only makes you feel as if you are right there with him, but also as if you are a most welcome companion

- Mary Lou Torre

These stories are written from the heart. The saying 'God is in the details' surely applies here, as Matthias takes us on a journey of the little things we often miss in our hurried culture. He gives us a sense of place, smell, sound, and taste. He writes with the eye of a photographer

- Sherry Karver

I just finished reading fish camping (with a glass of Sancerre, BTW). I realized that an appealing aspect of reading the sketches is that they engage my own travel memories, and it becomes a sort of time-delayed conversation. "Ah, yes, I remember that, and did you see...." and "oh, I've not been there, I must go back and visit." Since I lived in France for a year and a half in Paris trying to learn French, those French visits certainly resonate

- Carol Brownson

www.ingramcontent.com/pod-product-compliance
Lightning Source LLC
LaVergne TN
LVHW010304070426
835508LV00026B/3434